D1590579

THE
STORY
OF
CREATION

ALSO BY CALUM M. CARMICHAEL

The Origins of Biblical Law: The Decalogues and the Book of the Covenant

Law and Narrative in the Bible: The Evidence of the Deuteronomic Laws and the Decalogue

The Laws of Deuteronomy

Women, Law, and the Genesis Traditions

The Spirit of Biblical Law

THE
STORY
OF CREATION

Its Origin and Its
Interpretation in Philo
and the Fourth Gospel

Calum M. Carmichael

CORNELL UNIVERSITY PRESS

Ithaca and London

THIS BOOK HAS BEEN PUBLISHED WITH THE AID OF A GRANT
FROM THE HULL MEMORIAL PUBLICATION FUND OF CORNELL UNIVERSITY.

First published 1996 by Cornell University Press.

Library of Congress Cataloging-in-Publication Data

Carmichael, Calum M.
    The story of Creation : its origin and its interpretation in Philo and the
Fourth Gospel / Calum M. Carmichael.
        p.   cm.
    Includes bibliographical references and indexes.
    ISBN 0-8014-3261-8 (alk. paper)
    1. Bible. N.T. John I–V—Criticism, interpretation, etc.   2. Philo of
Alexandria.   3. Creation—Biblical teaching.   4. Bible. O. T.
Genesis I.1–II.4—Use.   I. Title.
BS2615.2.C364   1996
220.6—dc20   96-6131

Printed in the United States of America

♾ The paper in this book meets the minimum requirements of the
American National Standard for Information Sciences—Permanence of Paper
for Printed Library Materials, ANSI Z39.48-1984.

Contents

Preface   vii

Abbreviations   xi

1. The Origin of the Story of Creation   1

2. The Days of Creation in the Fourth Gospel   32

3. Day One   41

4. Day Two   56

5. Day Three   67

6. Day Four   79

7. Day Five   90

8. Day Six   99

9. Day Seven   115

Index of Sources   127

Subject Index   135

Preface

For centuries biblical texts have spawned the minor industry of hermeneutics, the science of interpretation. Indeed, much of modern literary criticism has its roots in biblical hermeneutics. In this book I demonstrate how biblical texts, which have for so long been the subject of interpretation by scholars, are themselves exercises in interpretation of other literary compositions. I argue that the story of creation in Genesis 1 represents the interpretation of other biblical texts, and that it in turn, hundreds of years later, played a major role in the composition of a New Testament text, namely, the first five chapters of the Fourth Gospel.

My aim is twofold: to show how the story of creation in Genesis 1 came to be written and how in the Fourth Gospel it was used to transform historical reporting about the life of Jesus into a cosmological scheme. I first explain how the author of the seven-day scheme of creation in Genesis 1 produces it in response to his reading of the exodus story. I then work out how the author of the Fourth Gospel uses the story of creation to present his interpretation of the life of Jesus.

We have, then, the story of creation coming into existence as a reading of the exodus story and certain episodes belonging to the initial part of the life of Jesus (John 1–5) being presented as a reading of the creation story. What is striking, but not surprising, about the two enterprises is how modes of reading change greatly with the passage of centuries. The author of the story of creation takes the history of the exodus (which is centuries old in his time), and in a commonsense, wholly intelligible way counters certain negative developments in it. By contrast, the author of the Fourth Gospel takes the story of creation and, by means of an allegorical method of interpreting Scripture that only the initiate in the culture he addresses can comprehend, produces his literary work on the life of Jesus. Central to the author's enterprise is Philo's method of working with Scripture, in particular, the creation story in Genesis 1. Philo, an Alexandrian Jew of the first century c.e., is the leading exponent of that form of Hellenistic Judaism which made scriptural teaching consonant with Greek philosophy, especially Platonic thought. It has long been recognized that the author of the Fourth Gospel owes much to Philo, but scholars have been reluctant to say in precisely what way. I argue that Philo's interpretation of the creation story is central to John's use of it.

My main goal is to show readers how rich and multifaceted is the business of interpretation in the ancient world; how, for example, literary activity can change dramatically with the passage of time even though the same focus, the nature of the created order, is the primary one; how enormous is the influence of a previous writing on the composition of a new piece; how a major influence on the first composition, the story of the exodus, is no longer known to the composer of the Johannine material; and how, in turn, the influence of the creation story of Genesis 1 has gone unrecognized by interpreters of John's Gospel.

I begin with a study of the account of creation in Genesis 1 and ask how it came to take the form it does. Comparable accounts of creation in the ancient Near Eastern world have proved disappointing in illuminating the special features and bias of Genesis 1. By relating Genesis 1 to the story of the exodus from Egypt, I attempt to solve problems—for example, why it takes the form of a seven-day scheme and why the climax is about a sabbath rest from work—which have long exercised other interpreters of the story of creation.

I then turn to John's Gospel and try a new way of explaining why it is such an impenetrable literary composition. It is often breathtaking to observe the literary artifice that went into his composition. In pursuit of his interpretive method I lay out a pattern of literary allusion that permits us to follow exactly the logic underlying his composition. John seems to proceed as if he is presenting a historical record that suggests to him certain philosophical and religious ideas. Quite the contrary has occurred. John takes certain ideas about the creation of the world from the account of creation in Genesis 1 and uses them to shape his historical narrative of events. The ideas determine the history, not history the ideas. Scholars have actually been aware of this phenomenon but never realized the extent to which it applies to John's writing, certainly not to his use of Genesis 1 in the first five chapters of his composition.

An example of John's artistry arises in a problem that scholars have long recognized: John's chronology in relation to the life of Jesus can differ markedly from the Synoptic chronology. The most dramatic example is that in the Synoptic Gospels Jesus dies on the first day of Passover, whereas in the Fourth Gospel he dies the day before Passover at the time of the sacrifice of the passover lamb. The Johannine date has been determined by his idea that Jesus should be identified with the passover lamb and the symbolic meaning attaching to it. (See R. E. Brown, *The Death of the Messiah* [New York, 1994], 1:845–48.) For John's interpretive purposes this identification determines the chronology. It is the religious idea that creates the history, not the history that primarily gives rise to the idea.

It is not just the Fourth Gospel that reveals this special interplay between ideas and history. The creation story in Genesis 1, while appearing to present a chronology of events, is in fact also an expression of religious ideas. The author creates the story of origins to communicate the idea of God's supremacy over man. The two stories of creation, Genesis 1 and John 1–5, exemplify to a remarkable degree what has come to be called intertextuality in modern literary studies. Each echoes, because there is a deliberate linkup with another writing, an earlier text, and each has been shaped by that earlier text.

I wish to express my indebtedness to Dale Allison, Friends

University, Wichita, Kansas; Oscar Brooks, Golden Gate Seminary, Mill Valley, California; Ernst Bammel and Norma Emerton, Cambridge University; W. D. Davies, Duke University; David Daube, University of California, Berkeley; David Winston, Graduate Theological Union Seminary, Berkeley; and John O'Neill, University of Edinburgh, for their helpful comments; also to my wife, Debbie, for her invaluable assistance with the writing of the manuscript.

The quotations from Philo of Alexandria are from the edition of the Loeb Classical Library. In quoting biblical texts I have relied on the King James Authorized Version of 1611 but made changes where these were called for. I have used the AV because it is in almost all cases a more literal rendering of the Hebrew and Greek manuscripts than any other translation. It also has the merit of reminding the reader of something I consider to be very important, namely, that biblical literature is a product of the past and hence of a culture quite different from our own.

CALUM M. CARMICHAEL

Ithaca, New York

Abbreviations

AB	Anchor Bible
Amoraite	A rabbi of the period of about 200 to 500 C.E.
AOAT	*Alter Orient und Altes Testament*
AV	Authorized Version
b.	Tractates in the Babylonian Talmud
Bar	Baruch
BAR	*Biblical Archaeology Review*
Barn.	Epistle of Barnabas
BNTC	Black's New Testament Commentary
BZ	*Biblische Zeitschrift*
CBQ	*Catholic Biblical Quarterly*
CBQMS	Catholic Biblical Quarterly Monograph Series
CBSC	Cambridge Bible for Schools and Colleges
CD	Cairo (Genizah text of the) Damascus (Document)
CSEL	Corpus Scriptorum Ecclesiasticorum Latinorum
D	The Deuteronomic literary strand in the Pentateuch
ET	English Translation
HBD	*Harper's Bible Dictionary*, ed. P. J. Achtemeier (San Francisco, 1985)
HJ	*Heythrop Journal*
HUCA	*Hebrew Union College Annual*
ICC	International Critical Commentary
JBL	*Journal of Biblical Literature*
JE	The Y(J)ahwistic and Elohistic literary strand in the Pentateuch

JEDP	The order of the literary strands in the Pentateuch
JJS	*Journal of Jewish Studies*
JLR	*Journal of Law and Religion*
JQR	*Jewish Quarterly Review*
JR	*Juridical Review*
JSNT	*Journal for the Study of the New Testament*
JSOT	*Journal for the Study of the Old Testament*
LAB	*Liber Antiquitatum Biblicarum*
LXX	The Septuagint
m.	Tractates in the Mishnah
NCBC	New Century Bible Commentary
*NT*Suppl.	*Novum Testamentum*, Supplements
NTS	*New Testament Studies*
OTL	Old Testament Library
P	The Priestly literary strand in the Pentateuch
RSV	Revised Standard Version
StTh	*Studia Theologica*
t.	Tractates in the Tosephtah
Tannaite	A rabbi of the period of about 50 B.C.E. to about 200 C.E.
VT	*Vetus Testamentum*
WC	Westminster Commentary
y.	Tractates in the Jerusalem Talmud
ZAW	*Zeitschrift für die alttestamentliche Wissenschaft*
ZNW	*Zeitschrift für die neutestamentliche Wissenschaft*

THE
STORY
OF
CREATION

Chapter 1

The Origin of the Story of Creation

Plainly, the story of creation in Genesis 1, like any contemporary scientific theory of origins, is a construction a goodly number of years after the fact.[1] Like so many biblical narratives, for example, the story of how Jacob (Israel) won out over Esau (Edom), it attempts to explain, even justify, why something has come to be as it is. The creation story is very much in line with the intense interest in origins that is exhibited in the rest of the Book of Genesis, for example, the origin of the fathers of the nation Israel.

A host of questions surrounds any inquiry into the origin and substance of Genesis 1. A well-recognized puzzle is why there are two stories recounting how creation came about (the ac-

---

1. David Daube once pointed out to me that the two recent theories of the origin of the universe have interesting analogues in past religious speculation about the origin of the world. In German Jewish circles at the turn of the century—from which background the theorist Hermann Bondi came—there was considerable controversy as to whether God created the world in six days and that was that, or whether, yes, something tremendous happened during these six days but God did not cease to create. The former view is similar to the Big Bang theory, the latter to the theory of Continuous Creation (associated with Bondi). The religious views on creation have a long history, to be found in Philo, the New Testament (Jn 5:16–36), and rabbinic sources; see Chapter 9. In two hundred years' time people will look back on contemporary theories and wonder how such speculations arose. Even if no religious influence is found to underlie them, the equally speculative views of science and religion will be cause for puzzlement.

count in Genesis 1 and the story of Adam and Eve). The two
stories are not reconcilable. For example, unlike the Adam and
Eve story, in which man is formed from the ground before the
animals (Gen 2:7, 19), the account of creation in Genesis 1
has the animals created before man. A related question is why
the two stories, with the Adam and Eve story coming second,
are arranged as they are.

A major question of substance specific to Genesis 1 is why
the model of a week of workdays followed by a day of rest is
the basis of its account of creation.[2] There is also the related
question why the day of rest, not the creation of the first humans, constitutes the climax of this account.

Research to date poses other questions. It is common to
study material from the ancient Near East to illuminate both
creation stories.[3] The consensus of scholarly opinion is that the
Akkadian myth of Atrahasis sheds some light on the substance
of the primeval history written up in Genesis 2–11 but that it
is less easy to come by an ancient Near Eastern source to illumine Genesis 1.[4]

While the creation stories reveal links of a general nature
with ancient Near Eastern sources, what we have to account for
are their distinctive Israelite features, for example, in Genesis 1,
the week of work followed by the day of rest. Are these features
illumined by other biblical material and, if so, are there specific reasons to explain the links?

There are such links, and three of them should be consid-

2. On the difference between the biblical sabbatical cycle and the Mesopotamian lunar cycle, see W. W. Hallo, "New Moons and Sabbaths: A Case-Study in
the Contrastive Approach," *HUCA* 48 (1977), 1–18. On the subject of workdays
and rest days in societies ancient and modern, see A. S. Diamond, *Primitive Law
Past and Present* (London, 1971), 354 n. 7.

3. See Claus Westermann's extensive study in *Genesis 1–11*, ET (Minneapolis,
1984), 19–47, 74–278; also B. F. Batto, "Creation Theology in Genesis," in *Creation in the Biblical Traditions*, ed. R. J. Clifford and J. J. Collins, CBQMS 24 (Washington, 1992), 31–38.

4. The Babylonian myth *Enuma Elish* may offer some illumination. A major
conclusion of Westermann (*Genesis 1–11*) is that "its [Genesis 1's] pre-history is
so broad and far-reaching that any derivation must remain questionable" (108).

ered. First, there is a connection between the account of creation in Genesis 1 and the construction of the Temple, which has been argued for by P. J. Kearney and Moshe Weinfeld.[5] Kearney sees a congruence between the six working days of Genesis 1, followed by the sabbath, and the development after the exodus from Egypt when God gave six commands in connection with the building of the tabernacle (Exod 25:1; 30:11, 17, 22, 34; 31:1), followed by the command about the sabbath (Exod 31:12–17).

Weinfeld is in favor of Kearney's observation but does not wish to uphold such a specific link. Instead, he focuses on Gen 1:1–2:3 (about the creation of the world) in relation to Exod 39:1–40:33 (about the construction of the tabernacle). He thinks these two accounts are typologically identical. "Both describe the satisfactory completion of the enterprise [the universe and the tabernacle respectively] commanded by God, its inspection and approval, the blessing and the sanctification which are connected with it. Most importantly, the expression of these ideas in both accounts overlaps."[6] Weinfeld explains his observations in the light of a relationship that he finds in the ancient Near East between traditions about the creation of the world and traditions about temple building. For example, in the Babylonian creation myth, *Enuma Elish,* after the creation was completed, the Temple Esagila was built for Marduk so that he could rest in it together with his retinue.

Second, there appears to be a concern with apostasy in Genesis 1. Gen 1:16 does not cite the sun and the moon by name. Commentators commonly speak of this curious omission as an indication that the author of Genesis 1 tacitly opposes a widespread belief in the ancient world that the heavenly bodies

5. P. J. Kearney, "Creation and Liturgy: The P Redaction of Ex 25–40," *ZAW* 89 (1977), 375–87; and Moshe Weinfeld, "Sabbath, Temple, and the Enthronement of the Lord—The Problem of the Sitz im Leben of Genesis 1:1–2:3," *Festschrift Cazelles, AOAT* 212 (1981), 501–12.

6. Weinfeld, "Sabbath," 503.

were divine and hence to be treated as objects of worship.[7] Texts such as Job 31:26–28 and Wis 13:2 openly condemn the practice.

Supporting this link between the creation story and apostasy is the Bible's frequent juxtaposition of God's creation of the world with the making of idols. The scorn heaped upon such enterprise and the idols themselves is commonplace, for example, Jer 10:1–16; Isa 40:12–14, 18–23, 45; Wisdom 13. At every turn the contrast is with the power exhibited by God in creating the heavens and the earth: "For thus saith Yahweh that created the heavens; God himself that formed the earth and made it; he hath established it, he created it not in vain, he formed it to be inhabited: I am Yahweh; and there is none else" (Isa 45:18).

Third, there is a link between the creation story of Genesis 1 and the exodus story. As far back as the Apocryphal Wisdom of Solomon, from around the beginning of the Christian Era, there is the view that the exodus brings about a re-creation of the world: "For the whole creation in its nature was fashioned anew [at the time of the exodus]" (Wis 19:6).[8]

There is no lack of evidence that the biblical writers themselves observed links between the topic of creation, on the one hand, and the drama of the exodus, on the other. Yahweh, having taken the Israelites by the hand to bring them out of Egypt, thinks of their future as he does of the fixed order of creation (Jer 31:31–37). Jeremiah praises Yahweh, who made the heavens and the earth by his great power and by his outstretched arm and who showed his signs and wonders in Egypt, bringing the Israelites out "with a strong hand and an outstretched arm" (Jer 32:17–21, cp. Amos 9:5–7). The notion of

7. See, e.g., S. R. Driver, *Genesis*, WC 6th ed. (London, 1907), 11; Gerhard von Rad, *Genesis*, OTL (London, 1961), 53, 54; Robert Davidson, *Genesis 1–11*, CBSC (Cambridge, Eng., 1973), 21; Westermann, *Genesis 1–11*, 127.

8. On the profound links drawn between the event of the exodus and the Genesis 1 account of creation in the Wisdom of Solomon, see Michael Kolarcik, "Creation and Salvation in the Book of Wisdom," in *Creation in the Biblical Traditions*, ed. Clifford and Collins, 97–107.

a new exodus after the pattern of the old one is a major motif in Second Isaiah, and it is typically linked to the power associated with the creation (Isa 41:17–20; 42:5–17; 43:15–21; 51:10). Psalm 136 first praises Yahweh for his work at creation, then for his work in bringing about the exodus. Exod 34:10 speaks of forthcoming marvels that God creates, comparable to the ones in Egypt (*nipla'ot* in Exod 34:10 and 3:20). In reference to the story of the exodus, Deut 4:32 states, "For ask now of the days that are past, which were before thee, since the day that God created man upon the earth, and ask from the one side of heaven unto the other, whether there hath been any such thing as this great thing [wonders at Sinai] is, or hath been heard like it?"

What is to be made of these links between the topic of creation, on the one hand, and the topics of temple construction, apostasy, and the exodus story, on the other? Nothing warrants us to assume that the topic of creation was so powerful and pervasive that it perforce permeates so many other topics. The ancient Israelites did not cultivate a philosophical and theological interest in the topic of creation such as occurs (as we shall see for Philo and John) in the intense cosmological speculations of later Jewish and Christian circles. Specific factors should be sought to explain the need to construct a story of creation as in Genesis 1.

One such factor may be some influence that comes from the surrounding Near Eastern cultural milieu. Babylonian mathematics provides the best example of a specific link between this milieu and other biblical material. They influenced the Priestly writers in working out their chronological schemes.[9] Alas, there is little or no trace of any comparable, specific influence at play in regard to Genesis 1.

9. For the remarkable link between Babylonian mathematics and biblical historiography, see the seminal articles by D. W. Young, "On the Application of Numbers from Babylonian Mathematics to Biblical Life Spans and Epochs," *ZAW* 100 (1988), 331–61, and "The Influence of Babylonian Algebra on Longevity among the Antediluvians," *ZAW* 102 (1990), 321–35.

A different factor—to be sure, general in nature—deserves attention. It is a truism that religions focus on how death, sickness, suffering, and sin came into the world rather than on the origin of what is pleasant and agreeable, the feature characteristic of the creation account in Genesis 1. The pleasant and the agreeable are generally taken for granted. When, however, the negative obtrudes on the pleasant, what goes without saying is then openly stated. We do not say of a clean person that he or she is undirty, thereby drawing attention to a negative quality. But we do refer to a dirty person as unclean because the negative of the positive quality that we take for granted is what catches our attention. That sexual activity occurred between a man and a woman was so taken for granted that it was not until about one hundred years ago that the word, "heterosexual," of a rather technical character, was coined to describe it. What, contrariwise, was perceived to be unpleasant and unacceptable in sexual relations, namely, between partners of the same sex, had a plethora of terms with a long history.[10]

This universal phenomenon may be relevant to the origin of the creation story in Genesis 1. By and large, it is taken for granted that the orderly and the positive prevail, for example, that the world is a good creation. Consequently, one should sit up and take notice when what is taken for granted, in this instance the orderly nature of a beneficent universe, is spelled out—as in Genesis 1. Negative factors may have prompted the author to spell out the positive nature of the created order. From this perspective it is less surprising that the grimness of the created order in Egypt at the time of the exodus, for example, may have engaged his attention in setting out a story of creation.

10. On the phenomenon in both language and law, see David Daube, "Intestatus," *Revue historique de droit français et étranger* 15 (1936), 341–43; "The Self-Understood in Legal History," *JR* 85 (1973), 126–34; "The Contrariness of Speech and Polytheism," *JLR* 11 (1995), 1601–5.

THE CREATION STORY AND THE STORY OF THE GOLDEN CALF (EXODUS 32)

For specific illumination of the creation story, it is sensible to look, not at the greater world of the ancient Near East, but at other biblical material. One feature of biblical literature that stands out above all others is its intense interest in origins. So many biblical narratives, not just the Book of Genesis, reflect this interest in universal and Israelite origins, narratives that stretch from the origin of the world in Genesis 1 to the origin of kingship in the Book of Samuel.[11] I wish to argue that there is a major, specific factor, not hitherto recognized, that accounts for the construction by the Priestly writer (P) of the creation story in Genesis 1. It is another biblical story about origins, namely, how the Israelites at the time of the exodus from Egypt resort to apostasy for the first time in their history. The people prompt Aaron to make a golden calf for them to worship as a god when Moses is absent for the purpose of receiving the decalogue (Exodus 32). The first instance in the nation's history of a man's fashioning a god inspires, I claim, the account of how God fashions the world.

One indication that this may be the correct line of inquiry to pursue is that the Priestly writers do in fact juxtapose the topic of the creation of the world according to Genesis 1 and the story of the golden calf. Just before the story of the calf is set down, Exodus 31, a Priestly composition that immediately precedes it touches on matters relating to the creation of the world. There is instruction about the observance of the sabbath and how the sabbath is a sign that God created the world in six days and rested on the seventh (Exod 31:17).

The story of the golden calf combines all four factors noted above that may be pertinent to an inquiry into the substance

---

11. On the crucial importance of this feature in the formulation of biblical legal material, see C. M. Carmichael, *The Origins of Biblical Law: The Decalogues and the Book of the Covenant* (Ithaca, 1992).

and origin of the creation story in Genesis 1. First, the construction of the golden calf is judged to be a negative development. Second, the story of its construction is about apostasy. Third, the story is recounted as an integral part of the exodus story. Fourth, it also involves the construction of an altar at which the golden calf is worshiped.

Right away we might note that the story of the golden calf did indeed give rise to speculation about such a fundamental matter as the nature of creation. Writers such as Hosea and the Psalmist view Aaron's creation in the following blunt terms: "The workman made it [the calf]: therefore it is not God" (Hos 8:6); "They made a calf in Horeb, and worshipped the molten image. Thus they changed their glory into the similitude of an ox that eateth grass" (Ps 106:20). For the Psalmist the notion of God's glory is integrally bound up with creation (Pss 19:2; 29:3; 108:6, cp. Isa 6:3).

In some ways the forging of a link between the making of the calf and the issue of the nature of creation is unexpected. The calf seems to represent but an image of Yahweh. Yet biblical interpreters came to view the calf as the setting up of a rival god to Yahweh. How this way of comprehending Aaron's action comes about is traceable. It is common to view the story of the calf in Exodus 32 in light of later political and religious history. At the time of the secession of King Jeroboam from the rule of the kingdom of Judah in Jerusalem (1 Kgs 12:25–33), the northern sanctuaries of Bethel and Dan install golden calves. Succeeding generations of the northern kings continue the practice. The calves symbolize the god Yahweh, who is worshiped in the southern kingdom of Judah at the Temple in Jerusalem.

Bull calves did exist in the Temple in the form of pedestals for the deity (1 Kgs 7:25, 44; 2 Chron 4:4, 15). Indeed, cosmic symbolism attached to them. As part of its iconography the Temple contained a bronze sea in the form of a bowl with twelve oxen supporting it. Equal numbers of these oxen pointed in each of the four directions of the universe, thus suggesting some cosmological significance.[12] The religious aim of the kings of northern Israel was to counter the attraction of the Temple at Jerusalem. The function the calves performed in the Jerusalem Temple could not, we might assume, be duplicated in the northern shrines. The possible consequence was that the figure of a calf took on an enhanced religious significance in these shrines.[13] Unfortunately, there is no way of telling whether the animal figures both in the Temple and in the northern shrines shared similar symbolical meaning. The related political aim of the northern kings was to prevent their subjects from traveling to Jerusalem and worshiping at the Temple and having them give their allegiance to the king of Judah.

From the perspective of the north-south tension in monarchical times, the story of the golden calf in Exodus 32 can be viewed as an etiological composition, an invention long after the fact, designed to condemn the political and religious positions of these northern kings. The story in Exodus 32 "proves" that the great lawgiver Moses himself condemned the use of the image of a bull calf in the worship of Yahweh.[14] To be sure, the story, as is true of many etiological compositions, probably has a historical basis. The role of the bull calves in the Jerusalem Temple is probably what inspired their being put to a different use in the northern shrines. Their assocation with the Temple would mean that they belonged to Israelite religious history and hence were associated with Aaron because he was the first of the priests. The problem for those who were opposed to the development in the northern kingdom would

12. See John Gray, *I and II Kings*, OTL (Philadelphia, 1963), 176–78.

13. In his article "Bull," in *HBD*, 144, R. J. Clifford is in no doubt that the young bulls that Jeroboam set up in Bethel and Dan represent the animal throne of Yahweh in the Jerusalem Temple and that consequently it became an object of worship.

14. For the parallels, some thirteen of them, between the two developments, see Moses Aberbach and Leivy Smolar, "Aaron, Jeroboam, and the Golden Calves," *JBL* 86 (1967), 129–40.

be how to reconcile the calves' association with Aaron. The story in Exodus 32 is the attempt to show that the significance attributed to the calves among these later kings had been discounted back in Aaron's time when he was involved in the beginnings of Israelite communal worship.[15]

In any event, the narrator who presents the story of the golden calf in Exodus 32 adopts a religious perspective that perceives and condemns Aaron's construction of the calf as an attempt by a human being to create God. While it may be true that both Aaron and Jeroboam simply wished to have Yahweh represented by the calf, the recorders of their histories do not maintain such a benign view.[16] They take the deeper implication that man could create God very seriously. They would have been all the more inclined to do so if the golden calves in the northern sanctuaries were indeed linked to the Temple oxen with their manifest cosmic associations.

The making of the golden calf can pose fundamental questions, namely, who creates what in this world and how is this creativity to be assessed? It raises the issue, I wish to argue, that requires the account of creation in Genesis 1. The motivation to take up the issue is a compelling one. Once Aaron's action was viewed as one in which man makes a god, it required the counteraffirmation that God created the world, certainly including humankind, such as Aaron, and animal kind, such as a calf. The topic of apostasy, in the form of the worship of the calf, then becomes very pertinent to the account of creation in

15. As B. S. Childs points out, the negative assessment of Aaron in Exodus 32 over against his positive role in other biblical traditions presents a major problem (*The Book of Exodus*, OTL [Philadelphia, 1974], 569–71).

16. Although any religious position has a political component, examples can be multiplied endlessly in which a religious position is primarily a cover for a political one. The Pharisaic dogma of the resurrection of the body is an example: the Sadducees, not acknowledging it, were thereby written out of Jewish religion and tradition. Early Christian opposition to contraception had a religious basis but was primarily politically motivated because of competition with gnostic developments. See John Noonan, *Contraception*, 2d ed. (Cambridge, Mass., 1986), 56–106.

Genesis 1 and strengthens the impression of such a link on the part of other interpreters.

The first tablet of the decalogue constitutes evidence that there exists a specific link between the topic of apostasy as it shows up in Exodus 32 and the substance of the Genesis creation story. The decalogue is itself an invented myth about the origin of divine law. God speaks in a setting in which elemental forces of creation accompany his pronouncements (Exodus 19). Among other manifestations of divine power, there is a voice from heaven, thunder and lighting, smoke and fire, and a descent of the deity upon the top of a mountain. In speaking his pronouncements God contemplates the future life of the Israelites. A major feature of biblical narrators and lawgivers is that they always focus on first-time developments in the history of the nation. The author of the decalogue focuses on the first outbreak of actual idolatry among the Israelites and consequently issues judgments on aspects of the offense of the making of the golden calf.

In stating at the opening of the decalogue that he is Yahweh their God who brought them out of Egypt, God is reacting against the claim made on behalf of the golden calf, namely, that it is the divine agency by which the people are brought out of Egypt (Exod 32:4). He next prohibits the worship of other gods in preference to him.[17] What is specifically in focus is the golden calf, spoken of as a plurality of gods by the people when they respond to its creation: "These are your gods, O Israel, who brought you up out of the land of Egypt" (Exod 32:4).[18] The people are not discounting Yahweh. After all, the calf is thought of as Yahweh. They are, however, acknowledging

17. The prepositional *'al-peney,* usually translated "before," has in fact the meaning "in defiance of, in preference to," as in, for example, Deut 21:16: a man has not to give a son by a loved wife the double share of his inheritance "before, in preference to" (*'al-peney*) a son by a hated wife who is his firstborn son.

18. The plurality of gods is probably taking into account the calves in the northern shrines of Bethel and Dan.

their own creation in preference to the Yahweh they have known in their dealings with Moses.

The divine prohibition against other gods spells out in more detail the kind of image that is in focus, namely, one that resembles something in heaven, earth, or the seas. In this amplification of what is meant by a graven image there is the threefold division of the universe that shows up in Genesis 1. This link, then, between the story of the calf and the nature of the created order is an indication that reflection on the making of the image of something on earth, the calf, generated wider thinking about the nature of the universe such as exists in Genesis 1.

The two following rules in the first tablet of the decalogue were set forth in similar reaction to the making of the calf, and again the topic of creation comes to the surface. Aaron builds an altar for the calf and calls it Yahweh when he sets aside a special day to hold a festival in its honor (Exod 32:5). His proclamation about this day has elicited the prohibition against using the divine name for a vain purpose, namely, by calling a dumb object, the calf, Yahweh. Likewise, Aaron's setting aside the special day to honor a man-made god has elicited the counterdemand that the Israelites set aside the sabbath day to honor the god who created the world.[19]

The rule about the sabbath day reveals a direct link with the creation story of Genesis 1. The rule refers to how God created in six days the heaven, earth, and seas, and all that is in them, and rested on the seventh day (Exod 20:11). This justification for keeping the rule about the sabbath has thus built into it the outline of the creation story in Genesis 1. The rule against the vain use of Yahweh's name in turn reveals an indirect link with Genesis 1. Aaron's proclamation, his wrongful use of the divine name Yahweh, means that he embraces the power of language associated with the name of God to honor a human creation. From this perspective Aaron usurps the power of lan-

19. For a detailed exposition, see Carmichael, *Origins of Biblical Law*, 22–50.

guage that is properly associated with the deity, for example, when in the creation story of Genesis 1 God's use of language was the power that brought about the creation of the world.

THE CREATION STORY AND THE EXODUS STORY

A link has long been noted to exist between the topic of creation and the exodus story. I wish to argue for a particular link between the story of Exodus 32 and the most distinctive feature of the creation story in Genesis 1, namely, six days of work followed by a day of rest. It is again important to focus on Aaron's special day when he sets it aside so that the people might celebrate a festival (*ḥag*, Exod 32:5) in honor of their golden calf Yahweh.

Aaron's special day is about the central issue of the exodus story because his festival represents the fulfillment—a wrongful one—of the explicitly stated goal of Moses' and Aaron's negotiations with the pharaoh. A divine oracle to Moses ("Thus says Yahweh")[20] made the demand to the pharaoh that he permit the Israelites to go to a festival (*ḥag*, Exod 5:1; 10:9) in the wilderness to celebrate their god.[21] On the occasion of Aaron's festival, in the wilderness, the people herald their god, the calf Yahweh, that had brought them out of Egypt (Exod 32:4). But this was the very occasion that the pharaoh opposed because from his stance it constituted a rest of the Israelites from their labor (Exod 5:5). The verb used for this rest from labor is

20. This same oracular expression is used again in Exod 32:27 when Moses has the loyal Levites punish those guilty for the offense of the calf. As Childs points out, the use of this prophetic idiom in the Pentateuch is rare (*Exodus,* 105, 571).

21. Although there is no indication in the text, it is conceivable that the festival in the wilderness spoken about by Moses and Aaron to the pharaoh is simply a ruse on their part to achieve liberation (cp. Exod 5:9). See S. R. Driver, *Exodus,* CBSC (Cambridge, Eng., 1911), 25. The important point is, however, not what the historical situation is but how later thinkers assessed the ideas and attitudes that emerged in the account of the exodus.

shabbat. On the occasion the pharaoh also denies knowing who Yahweh is, a situation that changes once Yahweh's power becomes known to him through the plagues. From the perspective of the negotiation with the pharaoh, and hence the aim of the exodus story, Aaron's special day—whatever actual day of the week it was is irrelevant—was Israel's sabbath rest, the one implied in the pharaoh's complaint, and on it the Israelites honored God, albeit Aaron's man-made god. S. R. Driver points out that there is "no indication or hint of its [the sabbath] being observed as such in pre-Mosaic times."[22] In other words, the origin of the institution of the biblical sabbath is bound up with the experience of the exodus.

The profound issues raised by the unique occasion of Aaron's festival in the wilderness after the exodus from Egypt provide the motivation for the account of creation in Genesis 1. Inspiring this account, I am arguing, is the judgment that Aaron's creation is not the God Yahweh and that his man-made god does not deserve a day in its honor.[23] This negative judgment occasioned the need to set down an account of creation that featured the creative actions of the true God—the invisible God of the exodus story who received a name that is from the verb "to be," that may in fact be the causative form of this verb, namely, *yahweh,* "he causes to be" (Exod 3:14).[24] And, most important, this opposing account, the story of creation, had to culminate in a day that celebrated the true God's creative acts, the legitimate day of rest, because his work on behalf of the Hebrew slaves was to the end that they could enjoy a

22. Driver, *Book of Genesis,* WC, 18.

23. The author of Genesis 1 uses the verb *bara'* ("to create"). Commentators, for example, Westermann, *Genesis 1–11,* 98, 99, point out that this verb always has Yahweh as its subject, as in the creation story of Genesis 1, and is never used with a preposition or an accusative of the material out of which God creates: "P wanted to say how entirely different was God's creative action from anything that humans can do." If this statement is accurate, the contrast in focus is God's role in creation as against Aaron's role in creating a god from gold.

24. For the linguistic form *yahweh* as a causative, see W. F. Albright, *From the Stone Age to Christianity* (Baltimore, 1940), 197–99. For other attempts to have the name refer to Yahweh as Creator, see Childs, *Exodus,* 60–64.

rest from their daily tasks in Egypt. What has to be pinned down is exactly how the link between the exodus story and the story of creation comes about.

The story of the exodus is patently about the unrelenting work of the Israelites in Egypt and their God's helpful response to the hardship experienced. He has them seek a break from their daily tasks so that they might celebrate a religious festival in the wilderness (Exod 3:18; 4:23; 5:1, 3; 8:1, 8, 20, 25–29; 9:1, 13; 10:3, 7–9, 24–26; 12:31). The pharaoh's response is negative because, as indicated, he interprets their request as a shirking of their daily tasks, as a desire to rest (*shabbat*) from their burdens (Exod 5:5). Many times the Israelites make the request to worship their god, but their request meets with frustration of one kind or another. Only after God performs many acts in opposition to the pharaoh's refusal to grant a rest from work are the Israelites released from their bondage in Egypt. Of any immediate celebration in the wilderness, however, along the lines of the Israelites' request to the pharaoh, there is no account.

To be sure, there is instituted the commemorative celebration of the Passover, but that is primarily intended to recall in the future life of the nation the dramatic events that bring about the final departure from Egypt (Exodus 12, 13). But no commemorative Passover is actually celebrated by the Israelites when they are in the desert. There is also the incident when Jethro, Moses' father-in-law, celebrates Yahweh's victory over the Egyptians with burnt offerings and sacrifices, but only the Hebrew nobles attend (Exod 18:8–12). It is not a celebration involving all the people. Thus neither the institution of the Passover nor Jethro's celebration would be considered the equivalent of the religious occasion that is constantly in focus in the negotiations with the pharaoh.

Eventually a religious celebration takes place in the wilderness. Moses is supposedly lost on the mountain and the people are in the care of Aaron. Not expecting to see Moses again, they request Aaron to make them gods whom they can acknowledge as their deliverers from bondage in Egypt and who

will go before them in their future travels (Exod 32:1, 4).
There then follows the apostasy involving the making of the
calf.

Whatever else it betokens, Aaron's man-made god symbolizes
Israel's rest from the labor of Egyptian slavery. The Priestly
author of Genesis 1 opposes, I am arguing, this understanding
of what takes place. He does so by paying attention to how the
God Yahweh is actually depicted in accomplishing the task of
bringing about the release from slavery. He might first have
observed that Aaron's day of celebration is preceded by a human wonder: "I [Aaron] cast it [gold] into the fire, and there
came out this calf" (Exod 32:24). It is usually assumed that
Aaron's comment about the wonder he produces is an attempt
by him to save face. It may, however, be much more than that,
namely, the suggestion that he is claiming a unique ability to
create.

For the Priestly writer it is Yahweh's wonders on behalf of
the Israelites in Egypt that prove he is the true Yahweh, not
the work of Aaron in crafting a calf, calling it Yahweh and
claiming its power brought them out of Egypt (Exod 32:4).
The Priestly author's concern with Yahweh's power exhibited
in Egypt and the end result to which it is directed, relief from
labor, is a primary source of inspiration for the composition of
the creation story. Just as the Israelites should set aside a day
to enjoy rest from work in commemoration of their hardship
in Egypt—as the sabbath command in Deut 5:12–15 spells out
explicitly—so on the same day there should be commemoration of a series of events, namely, those of creation, that constituted the necessary prerequisite for Yahweh's actions on
behalf of the Israelites in Egypt. Without the events of the initial creation of the world there could, in the nature of things,
be no exploitation of their consequences to bring about the
deliverance of the Israelites from their hardship in Egypt. I
shall shortly point out how the developments in the exodus
story invite reflection about the nature of the created world.

Aaron's depiction of how he used fire to bring forth a golden calf that he then proclaimed to be the power behind the events of the exodus brings up the fundamental issue of ultimate capacity to create. When Aaron attributes significance to the calf as the agent responsible for bringing about the exodus, his basis for doing so is his unique act of creating the calf from fire. By contrast, Yahweh's claim to be this same agent has its basis, so the author of Genesis 1 infers, I am claiming, in his unique role as the creator of the universe itself. In other words, the author of Genesis 1 reacts to Aaron's claim, directs his attention to Yahweh's role in the events of the exodus, and sees that power as necessarily dependent on the notion that Yahweh is the creator of the universe.

Yahweh's work in Egypt constitutes wonders, miracles of nature, and embraces all, or almost all, of the created order—and this point should be emphasized—as it is depicted in Genesis 1. He is the Yahweh of the "mighty hand and stretched out arm," involved with water, animals, insects, reptiles (Exod 7:9, 10, the *tanninim* of Gen 1:21), land (in the form of dust),[25] plants and fruit trees (Exod 10:15, the same distinction as in Gen 1:12), darkness (for the Egyptians), light (for the Israelites), and humankind (the firstborn). After the wonders of Egypt he produces a cloud by day and fire by night, and he makes the sea dry land. All in all these wonders represent "the great work [hand] of Yahweh" (Exod 14:31).[26]

I am suggesting that the author of the creation story in Genesis 1 set himself the task of transforming the chaotic forces on display in Egypt into the orderly forces established at the creation of the world. These chaotic forces in Egypt are not random and uncontrolled but have a purpose behind them.

25. Cp. Gen 3:19: dust and ground are parallel terms; see Ziony Zevit, "The Priestly Redaction and Interpretation of the Plague Narratives in Exodus," *JQR* 66 (1975–76), 203 n. 35.

26. So Driver, *Exodus*, 121, who points out that the term "hand" is figurative for "act" or "work," as also in Deut 34:12 and Ps 78:42 to indicate again the works of God in Egypt and during the exodus.

Such a deliberate use implied that they had been diverted from their usual role. Consequently, what takes place invited speculation as to what the order of creation is.

This process of wondering what lay behind the chaos in Egypt explains why T. E. Fretheim can argue that the theme of creation is indeed paramount in the Exodus narrative.[27] The one major problem with his argument, which must be kept in mind in assessing his position, is that he ignores the standard view that the P creation story of Genesis 1 is a much later composition than the mainly JE story of the exodus. Fretheim's views are nonetheless worth noting so long as one remembers that the creation story is the obverse of the exodus story, not the other way around as he seems to believe.[28]

For Fretheim the narrator of the exodus views Pharaoh's oppressive measures as antilife and anticreation. There is, Fretheim claims, an allusion in Exod 1:7, "The land was filled with them [the Israelites]," to Gen 1:28, 29, the blessing on the human beings in the creation story to be fruitful and multiply. Pharaoh's measures against the growth of Israel's populace "strike right at the point where the creational promise of fruitfulness is being fulfilled in Israel."[29] The pharaoh's actions represent the return of the forces of chaos that were overcome at the creation of the world. His actions in turn trigger reactions by the Israelite deity that add to this chaos. The plague of darkness in Exod 10:21–29, for example, is a reversion to a precreation state. The devastating effects of every plague are such that every sphere of the created order is adversely affected.[30]

27. T. E. Fretheim, "The Plagues as Ecological Signs of Historical Disaster," *JBL* 110 (1991), 385–96.

28. His view is the traditional one expressed in Wis 19:6: "For the whole creation in its nature was fashioned anew [at the time of the exodus]."

29. Fretheim, "Plagues," 385. Fretheim speaks of the creational command of Gen 1:28, 29, of Israel having fulfilled it. But it is not a command, only a blessing, just as "Have a nice day" is a blessing, not a command. On the fundamental importance of the distinction, see David Daube, *The Duty of Procreation* (Edinburgh, 1977), 3, 4, 41, 42.

30. For a link between the creation of the world and plagues, note 2 Macc 7:23, 28, 37.

The continuous use of the word "all" (*kol*) shows that nothing in the entire earthly order escapes. The deliverance of Israel is ultimately for the sake of the entire creation, and this view, according to Fretheim, explains the significance of such texts as Exod 8:22; 9:14, 16, 29 which claim that the earth belongs to Yahweh.

Fretheim may well be right in arguing that from the perspective of the present form of the Pentateuch (the Priestly redaction), the story of the exodus is to be read as a description of how "God's work in and through Moses, climaxing in Israel's crossing of the sea on 'dry land,' constitutes God's efforts of re-creation, to return creation to a point where God's mission can once again be taken up"[31] Fretheim is thinking of the watery chaos that preceded the emergence of the earth in the creation story. At the time of the plagues the appearance of the infected water, the frogs, the dust and the gnats, the flies, the epidemic among cattle, the ashes and the boils, the weather phenomena, the locusts, and darkness all constitute distortions of what had been created by God. Water is no longer simply water; light and darkness are no longer separated; the people are diseased, the animals run amok, the insects and amphibians swarm out of control. Fretheim implies that the plagues that are bad stand in sharp contrast to the good things that happened at creation.

Fretheim avoids the issue of source criticism and consequently does not discuss the question how the idea about the cosmic aspect of the chaos in Egypt arose. If the P story of creation is much later than the JE account of the exodus, the transmission of ideas underlying the final form of the text cannot be as traditionally thought: first the story of the creation, then a reversion to the preexisting chaos in the exodus narrative, and then to re-creation. Rather the line of development is first the exodus with its theme of chaos of almost cosmic proportions and then the creation story with its theme of order

31. Fretheim, "Plagues," 392–93.

and benevolence. To be sure, once composed, the P story of
creation might well have influenced and brought out even
more—along the lines that Fretheim describes—the cosmic
bias in the presentation of Israel's geographically localized experience in Egypt. There is evidence of a P redaction of the
exodus story. For example, the texts in Exod 1:7 and Gen
1:28, 29 about the multiplication of human beings both come
from P.[32]

Fretheim's further observations on the Book of Exodus provide two examples of how one of its narratives incorporates and
transforms a negative feature of a preceding one. The process
in question might furnish some insight into, possibly even be
a model for, how on a grander scale the creation story came
to transform the negative side of the exodus story. Fretheim
observes how the plagues in Egypt have their reverse analogues
in the aftermath of the exodus. He speaks of these reversals as
"God's re-creational activity."[33] As a consequence of the first
plague in Egypt the water could not be drunk (Exod 7:24). In
Exod 15:23 the Israelites are in a similar situation, but the
undrinkable water is made sweet and the wilderness itself
is filled with springs of water.[34] In Exod 9:18, 23, God rains
(*mṭr*) hail upon Egypt, and it destroys the sources of food. In
Exod 16:4 there is the opposite situation: God rains (*mṭr*) bread
from heaven to relieve the starvation of the Israelites in the
wilderness.[35] Both these accounts are attributed to the J and E
traditions, but interestingly P's contribution makes an appearance.[36]

32. See Westermann, *Genesis 1–11*, 140.

33. Fretheim, "Plagues," 395.

34. For the importance in the history of medicine of the curative process exhibited in this story, see David Daube, "Example and Precept: From Sirach to R.
Ishmael," *Talmudic Law*, ed. C. M. Carmichael (Berkeley, 1992), 205–11.

35. The expression in Exod 16:15, "to give for food" (*le'aklah*) is a fixed
Priestly formula—some seven times in the Priestly writing—and is the one used
in Gen 1:29. See Westermann, *Genesis 1–11*, 162.

36. On the redaction of these two stories, see Childs, *Exodus*, 266, 275. The
repetitions of theme are but a characteristic of the presentation of many another
matter in the Pentateuch, for example, the usurpation of the firstborn in the

From a critical viewpoint the direction of thought in these two examples of reversal of fortune (the water and the food) is from the contemplation of the chaos in Egypt to a heightened perception of the nature of creation, in particular, to a perception that creation can be viewed as benevolent. It is a movement of thought that is similar to, I am claiming, what occasioned the systematic P account of the good creation in Genesis 1.[37] The negative development in another postexodus happening, namely, the making of the golden calf, is the catalyst that triggered this end result. In the Song of the Sea in Exodus 15, as Fretheim points out, the divine victory over the powers of chaos assumes cosmic proportions, and it contains language about creation. This composition (possibly J) is much older than the P story of creation and reveals the trend of thought that has gone into the composition of the P creation narrative.

Although it is not possible to be privy to exactly what prompted the Priestly author of Genesis 1 to construct his material as he does, there are at least some hints as to how he proceeded. Nine such indications, some more specific, some more persuasive than others, might be considered.

One, there is the threefold division of the universe that emerges in the decalogue, which, I argued, came from a generalizing reflection on the role of the image of an animal, the bull calf, in Aaron's activity in Exodus 32. The apostasy has

---

successive families of Abraham, Isaac, Jacob, and Joseph; famine in Joseph's Egypt, in the Egypt of the pharaoh at the time of the exodus, and in the wilderness after the departure from Egypt. Central to the treatment of the manna story of Exodus 16 in Philo and in ancient Judaism (*Mek.* on Exod 16:4) is the notion of the inversion of the original order of creation. Philo speaks of how the food given from heaven follows the analogy of the birth of the world (*Mos.* 2.267).

37. The first account of the Israelites' receiving instruction in sabbath observance comes from the largely P story of the giving of the manna in the wilderness during the exodus (Exodus 16). On the occasion the Israelites receive a miraculously exact portion of food each of six days. On the sixth day they receive twice the amount to suffice them for the seventh day, on which they are to rest. In the creation story the arrangement to feed humankind was followed immediately by the act of the creation of the sabbath (Gen 1:29–2:3).

provoked P's thoughts about creation. The prophet Jeremiah provides a prior example of similar reflection. In lamenting Israel's apostasy, Jeremiah conjures up a primeval chaos: "I beheld the earth, and, lo, it was without form, and void; and the heavens, and they had no light" (Jer 4:23).

Two, in Deut 32:11 (cp. Exod 19:4) the Deuteronomist employs a metaphor about how Yahweh hovers over the Israelites like an eagle to protect them in the aftermath of the exodus, namely, in the wilderness, which is referred to as a "waste" (*tohu*), the term used of the chaos in Gen 1:2.[38] The use of this metaphor about the eagle may underlie the curious use of the verb "to hover" (*rhp*) in reference to the Spirit of God that "hovered over" the watery chaos on day one of creation. The verb occurs only in Gen 1:2 and Deut 32:11. The imagery about the hovering eagle describes how Yahweh is alone with Israel in the wilderness and how there is no foreign god with him (v. 12). As I have stressed, the topic of apostasy is relevant to the thinking underlying the creation story in Genesis 1.

Three, because of the elevation of the golden calf to a major role in the exodus story, the author of Genesis 1 would be opposed to any notion of a visible agent that was at work in the creation of the world. The reference to the Spirit of God that moved over the face of the primeval waters is consistent with such opposition. The Spirit is an unseen force.

Four, God creates by speaking. This feature may derive from the contrast with the dumbness of idols (Jer 10:5), in particular this attribute of the golden calf.[39] The prophet Isaiah, in an attack on the making of an idol, states, "To whom then will ye liken God? or what likeness will ye compare unto me?" (Isa 40:18). Isaiah then describes the making of a graven image and

---

38. "There is no sign of either personification or mythological allusion in the biblical use of *tohu*" (Westermann, *Genesis 1–11*, 103).

39. The agency of speech in the act of creation may also owe something to an awareness in some form of, for example, the Memphite cosmogony in which the Egyptian god Ptah creates in similar fashion. See John D. Currid, "An Examination of the Egyptian Background of the Genesis Cosmogony," *BZ* 35 (1991), 18–40.

discounts its significance by invoking the perspective of all creation and its creator (Isa 40:18–31). This perspective and this contrast are, I am suggesting, what determine the presentation of the Priestly account of creation in Genesis 1.

Five, there is Aaron's inappropriate, idolatrous naming of the calf Yahweh. In Gen 1:16 the deity's not naming the sun or the moon because of their presumed idolatrous significance stands in sharp relief to Aaron's giving a divine name, Yahweh, to the calf. Aaron gives a sacred name to a human creation. The Priestly writer has God refrain from giving names to two of his divine creations because he anticipates that their names will be infused with wrongful religious associations. The issue of God's giving or not giving names to what he created may therefore be more interesting than has hitherto been realized. The idolatrous worship of the sun, moon (and stars) is in fact linked to the worship of the calf in Deut 4:15–19.

Six, the description of the plague of darkness that comes when Moses stretches out his hand to heaven and that lasts three days does not refer to the sun or the moon (Exod 10:21–23). Conceivably, the odd idea that appears in Gen 1:2–5—both darkness and light issued forth from some hidden, mysterious place and the light was not derived from the sun—may come from reflection on this aspect of the exodus story.

Seven, the final plague in Egypt, the destruction of the human firstborn of the Egyptians, may account for the final item in the catalog of what came to be created, namely, humankind. The Adam and Eve story has humankind placed in a different order in its scheme of creation.

Eight, there is an obvious contrast between the grim nature of the cosmos at the time of the exodus—with only an indication of a move in a more positive direction—and the wholly positive work of creation in Genesis 1. In Egypt destruction is the order of the day. At least this is true so far as the Egyptians are concerned, but the negative effect extends to the Israelites because of the consequences, for example, the hardening of the pharaoh's heart that worsens their state of slavery. As Fretheim has pointed out, the effect of the plagues even extends to the whole creation. In the wilderness after the departure from Egypt the negative aspect of things shows up. There is no water and no food. The contrast between the nature of the created order at the exodus and that at the beginning of the world may account for the curious and repeated valuation put upon the works of creation in Genesis 1 that each in turn was good.[40]

Nine, there is in Genesis 1 the major input from the exodus story of the struggle of the Israelites to achieve a rest from their labors in Egypt. The author of Genesis 1 takes over the model of the week of work followed by a rest day from the particular way in which this struggle comes to a climax with Aaron's special day.

The story of creation in Genesis 1 is primarily a response to the making of the golden calf in Exodus 32—together with a focus on the rest from labor that the pharoah fears the Israelites will take should they hold a religious celebration in the desert, as Aaron and company in fact do when they worship the golden calf. Exodus 32 reveals other links with narratives in the Book of Genesis. That is, its link with Genesis 1 is not the sole example. For instance, in Moses' plea to God not to destroy the people (Exod 32:11–13) he recalls God's oath made with Abraham (Gen 22:16), the only place in Genesis where an oath confirms the covenant. Such a link involves a positive aspect of God's relation to Israel. Moses needs the deity's promise not to destroy the people in order to oppose God's anger over the calf.

Just as Genesis 1 is about beginnings, so the idea of beginnings also shows up in the story of the calf. God intends to wipe out the Israelites, with the exception of Moses, and begin over again, in this instance, to remake the nation. The offense that prompted such a sentiment has, I am arguing, also

40. Westermann unconvincingly argues that both in the Old Testament and in Mesopotamian and Sumerian myths the notion of praise of God by his creatures has become in Genesis 1 the reflection of God on his own creation (*Genesis 1–11*, 166).

prompted the need to set out the very beginnings of the created order. What causes a change of mind about the offense concerning the calf is the appeal to God's reputation in light of likely Egyptian scorn at his bringing the Israelites out of Egypt to destroy them "from the face of the earth" (Exod 32:12). In appealing to Abraham and the other patriarchs, Moses mentions how God's promise was to "multiply their descendants like the stars of heaven" (Exod 32:13). The language of creation is prominent in this appeal, and what is really asked for is the maintenance of God's reputation as the one who holds power over all creation.

THE CREATION STORY AND THE CONSTRUCTION OF THE TEMPLE

The placement of both Exodus 32, the story of the golden calf, and Genesis 1, the story of creation, in the Pentateuch proves revealing in light of the above observations. Consider, first, that Exodus 32 is related in the context of a section of P material just after the completion of instructions to Moses about the building of the tabernacle and an injunction about the observance of the sabbath (Exodus 31). P. J. Kearney and Moshe Weinfeld argued that there is a discernible link between the story of creation and the construction of the Temple. Whatever larger influences may be at work from the Near Eastern world—for example, the fundamental notion that the divine creator sought a residence on earth in the form of a temple—I would point to specific, internal reasons why the biblical material reveals the congruences both Kearney and Weinfeld detect.

There had to be a description of the proper way to worship Yahweh in the very context in which Aaron's errant way, the worship of the calf, is described. Furthermore, there also had to be instruction about the proper day to honor Yahweh in the very context in which Aaron set aside his improper day to honor the calf Yahweh. Why, then, is there an overlap between the description of the creation of the world and the building of the tabernacle? The answer is that Aaron's work of creating a god had to be opposed by God's work on creation; and Aaron's construction of an altar for his god had to be opposed by God's instructions about building the tabernacle. The description in Exod 31:2–11 of how the Spirit of God is imparted to the workman Bezalel to devise artifacts for the formal worship of Yahweh counters the action of the workman Aaron, who without God's sanction constructs an altar for his man-made god. Aaron's creation of god and his construction of an altar for its worship is what accounts for the symmetry of theme and presentation that Kearney and Weinfeld observe.

THE TWO STORIES OF CREATION IN GENESIS 1–3

A good deal can also be said about the placement of the creation story of Gen 1:1–2:4, namely, just before the story of Adam and Eve. In previous publications,[41] I have argued that the origin of the decalogue as a literary unit owes its inspiration to a compiler's focus on first-time developments in the history of Israel's life as a nation (the first tablet) and Israel's origin from the first human beings, Adam and Eve (the second tablet). Aaron's construction of the calf constitutes the first incident of idolatry in Israel's history, and each item of the decalogue up to the sabbath command makes a judgment on an aspect of the incident. Together the items constitute the first tablet of the decalogue. Each item after the sabbath command refers to the problems of human conduct experienced in the first family ever, Adam, Eve, Cain, and Abel, and together these items constitute the second tablet.

The decalogue's compilation is a product of the Deuteronomic literary activity in working with national traditions, an activity taken up and overlaid by the Priestly redaction of the

41. See C. M. Carmichael, *Law and Narrative in the Bible* (Ithaca, 1985), 313–42; *Origins of Biblical Law*, 22–45.

Pentateuch. The Deuteronomic version of the sabbath command has noted that the Israelites celebrated the calf as the
divine agent responsible for bringing Israel out of Egypt (Exod
32:4). Its version consequently has the Israelites recall that it
was Yahweh who brought them out (Deut 5:12–15). The
Priestly version, from another angle, noting that Aaron's day
of celebration for the calf Yahweh was in honor of a god created by a human being, opposed such a development by affirming Yahweh as the creator of the world (Exod 20:8–11).

The Priestly formulation of the sabbath command represents
the same kind of condemnatory reaction to the incident of the
golden calf as does the Priestly story of creation in Genesis 1.
Probably at the same time that the Priestly writer reformulated
the sabbath command, he composed the story of creation in
Genesis 1. He also placed his account of creation before the
other (JE) story of creation about Adam and Eve. He did so
because, in line with the opposition to the ideas that underlie
the creation of the calf, he found that the story of Adam and
Eve reveals the same problem of human aspiration to godlike
capacity: "Behold the man has become as one of us [the
gods]" (Gen 3:22). By setting down his account first, the
Priestly writer established an unbridgeable gulf between divine
beings and human beings. His account consequently served as
a bulwark against the compromise of Yahweh's power that
comes out in the Adam and Eve account.

With this view of the various texts in focus, one in line with
the JEDP hypothesis, better sense can be made of some longstanding puzzles. First, the two stories of creation are not
reconcilable, and in light of my argument this becomes intelligible. While on the one hand the Adam and Eve story could
be used to uncover the deity's moral code for the future governance of human conduct, on the other hand the story
needed a counterbalancing one to emphasize the transcendent
character of the deity in relation to humankind. The tension
between the two stories contains a contrast that permits each
story to communicate different matters. The first (Priestly)
story is, if only secondarily, composed by way of addressing

problems that arise in the second because in it the deity's involvement with Adam and Eve inevitably introduced an undesirable anthropomorphic character to the deity's role. The problem with such anthropomorphizing is precisely that human beings create gods according to their own conceptions, and this tendency is but a short step from the creation of physical images representative of divinity.

Second, there is an explanation for the sequence of the two stories of creation. The key is the recognition that the Priestly story of creation represents a reaction to the incident of the calf. The Priestly story was set down alongside the story of Adam and Eve but given priority of position, and the result was a sequence parallel to the one found in the decalogue. The original (Deuteronomic) decalogue was a composition inspired by the lawgiver's reaction first to the story of the calf and then to the story of Adam and Eve.

The congruence between the sequence of the two creation stories and the sequence of the two tablets of the decalogue accounts for the themes and language shared by the first story of creation and the first tablet of the decalogue. There is, for example, the obvious contrast between the condemnation in the first part of the decalogue of the creation of anything that resembles what is "in heaven above, or that is in the earth beneath, or that is in the water under the earth" (Exod 20:4) and the affirmation in the first story of creation that God created the heaven, the earth, and the seas (Gen 1:1–10). There is the contrast too between the condemnation of the human use of the divine name, again in the decalogue's first tablet, for something, the calf, judged to be unreal in how it was to function (Exod 20:7), and the affirmation in the first story of creation that God named most of the various entities that he had created and that had appropriate roles and functions ascribed to them. Again too, the first part of the decalogue and the first story of creation share a focus on the sabbath. In fact, the sabbath constitutes the last item in each composition.

Third, the ten pronouncements of the decalogue (Exod 34:28; Deut 4:13; 10:4) account for the ten pronouncements of God at the creation of the world. A characteristic of the Priestly writer is his interest in numbers and schemes of numbers, for example, the enumeration of the seven days of creation in Gen 1–2:3. It was he who took stock of the fact that the decalogue had ten pronouncements. When composing his account of creation he took over the feature of a pronouncement by God and sought to parallel the fact that there were ten such. After all, seven pronouncements of creation might have been expected because of the scheme of the seven days of creation.

The view that there were ten pronouncements at creation is found as early as *Pirqe Aboth* 5:1, "By ten sayings was the world created." The observation is presumably derived from noting the use ten times of "And God said," for example, "Let there be light." That the tenfold use of the formula in Genesis 1, "And God said," is a borrowing from the decalogue, and not the other way around, might be indicated by the fact that no internal or external feature of the decalogue suggests why there should be ten pronouncements. There just happen to be ten. It was the Priestly writer who chose to make something of the fact that there were ten pronouncements of the decalogue by duplicating this number in the attribution of ten words of creation to God.

For the creatures of sea and air in Gen 1:22 the formula used is "And God blessed them, saying, Be fruitful, and multiply," not "And God blessed them, and God said unto them, Be fruitful, and multiply," the formula used for the human beings in Gen 1:28. The reason for the avoidance of the formula "And God said" in Gen 1:22 may be that the Priestly writer wanted to have ten sayings, not eleven, to correspond to the ten sayings of the decalogue.[42]

---

42. Curiously, there is no corresponding blessing to be fruitful and multiply for the land animals. No doubt, it has to be inferred. Its omission means that no attention is focused upon their capacity to reproduce. It is probably unlikely, however, that the intention was to downplay the land animals because so much power was ascribed to the replica of one, the golden calf, in Israelite religion. Other interpreters see a problem too. Westermann, for example, thinks that the text may have been disturbed (*Genesis 1–11*, 141). Unlike the Adam and Eve story

The features of the narrative in Exodus 19 about the circum-
stances in which God gives the decalogue become more intelligible in light of the link between the decalogue and the story
of creation in Genesis 1. First, the exhibition of the elemental
forces of nature in Exodus 19 is consistent with a focus on
creation. Second, the descent of God to the earth on the third
day after the people assemble at the foot of the mountain recalls that it was on the third day of creation that the earth came
into existence. Third, the requirement that neither humans
nor animals come near the sacred site is by way of preparing
for the descent of God on the third day on the mountain. In
the sequence of the days of creation in Genesis 1 neither animal nor human life had appeared by the third day.

The setting in Exodus 19 for the pronouncements of the
decalogue re-creates the setting at the origin of the world in
Genesis 1. The consequence is that the voice that speaks at
Sinai is an echo of the voice whose pronouncements created
the world. This feature of the same voice that spoke on both
occasions accounts for the unique fact that only for the giving
of the decalogue does God speak his rules directly. Ordinarily
God communicates them through his intermediary Moses.

One of the most puzzling features of the giving of the decalogue is that a plain reading of the text of Exodus 19 leaves
the reader with no indication of the audience for its reception.
Critics have to resort to drastic textual surgery to solve the puzzle. They transpose, to just before the giving of the decalogue,
the text of Exod 20:18–21 about the terrifying effect of the
supernatural activity on the mountain and the request by the
people to Moses that God should not communicate to them

---

in which man is formed from the ground before the animals (Gen 2:7, 19), the
Priestly account of creation has the animals created before man. It follows that
the idea that a man could create God in the form of an animal is impossible
because living animals were created before he was. In other words, one should
not accept the common view that the creation of humankind is the climax of
creation—hardly convincing because the sabbath patently enjoys this distinction—but rather view man's creation by God in light of the author's intention to
downplay man's creative abilities as compared to the deity's.

directly but only through Moses.[43] The matter of audience is less puzzling if there is an attempt to suggest that the voice that spoke when creating the world, when there was no human audience to hear God's pronouncements, is the same voice that speaks on Sinai.

43. See J. P. Hyatt, *Exodus*, NCBC (Grand Rapids, 1971), 203, 217.

Chapter 2

The Days of Creation in the Fourth Gospel

Some of the ideas that are expressed in the Prologue to the Fourth Gospel recall the account of creation in the Book of Genesis.[1] For example, the light that shines in the darkness is reminiscent of the light that separates from the darkness at the opening of the creation story. Nonetheless, despite John's explicit reference to creation ("In the beginning was the Word"), his use of the Genesis text is not especially transparent

---

1. The Prologue in Jn 1:1–18 reads:
[1]In the beginning was the Word, and the Word was with God, and the Word was God. [2]The same was in the beginning with God. [3]All things were made by him; and without him was not any thing made that was made. [4]In him was life; and the life was the light of men. [5]And the light shineth in darkness; and the darkness comprehended it not. [6]There was a man sent from God, whose name was John. [7]The same came for a witness, to bear witness of the Light, that all men through him might believe. [8]He was not that Light, but was sent to bear witness of that Light. [9]That was the true Light, which lighteth every man that cometh into the world. [10]He was in the world, and the world was made by him, and the world knew him not. [11]He came unto his own, and his own received him not. [12]But as many as received him, to them gave he power to become the sons of God, even to them that believe on his name: [13]Which were born, not of blood, nor of the will of the flesh, nor of the will of man, but of God. [14]And the Word was made flesh, and dwelt among us, and we beheld his glory, the glory as of the only begotten of the Father, full of grace and truth. [15]John bare witness of him, and cried, saying, This was he of whom I spake, He that cometh after me is preferred before me: for he was before me. [16]And of his fulness have all we received, and grace for grace. [17]For the law was given by Moses, but grace and truth came by Jesus Christ. [18]No man hath seen God at any time; the only begotten Son, which is in the bosom of the Father, he hath declared him.

to a modern reader. One reason for this lack of transparency can be attributed to the rich and complex cluster of ideas with which John constantly works in presenting his material. The interconnected patterns of thought in John and the attendant difficulty of interpretation is a commonplace in biblical criticism. We should persist, however, in evaluating the relationship between the Johannine ideas on creation and the Genesis account because of at least three considerations.

First, John states that the Word, the Logos,[2] was not just present at creation, but brought it about (Jn 1:3; cp. Heb 1:2; Col 1:16, 17; Rev 3:14). Jesus is identified with the Word. A connection between Jesus' activity at creation and his historical deeds is therefore a possibility that we might consider.[3] We might find that the theme of creation appears not just at the opening of the Gospel in the Prologue but also in subsequent parts of it.

Already in the Prologue John switches back and forth between the account of Jesus as the preexistent Word at creation, references to the historical life of Jesus, and to John the Baptist's activity. Since John (the Gospel writer) combines the themes of Jesus' historical life and his existence at creation ("He was in the world, and the world was made by him, and the world knew him not" [1:10]), it might not have been too much of a leap for John to think of Jesus' life as somehow recapitulating the initial function of the Logos at creation. Other figures who appear in the Gospel might fit into this scheme, for example, John the Baptist. In the Prologue he

2. Although John takes over the Hellenistic notion of the logos as the creative and rational principle of the universe, it is clear that his fundamental position is that of a Jewish way of thinking. Thus when John has Jesus as "the Word made flesh," he goes on to state that no human being has seen God at any time, that only a manifestation, his begotten son, can be seen. The result is that a Hellenistic philosophical doctrine has been overlaid by a thoroughly rabbinic notion.

3. Compare how in the apocalyptic literature, the Enoch literature "is pervaded with the sense that human destiny is bound up with the order of the cosmos" (*Creation in the Biblical Traditions*, ed. R. J. Clifford and J. J. Collins, CBQMS 24 [Washington, 1992], 14).

bears witness to the light. We should be alert to a role for the Baptist in the subsequent account of his activity in the Gospel that might correspond to some role associated with Jesus on day one of creation, the day on which the original light was separated from the darkness.

Second, Johannine references to Old Testament material are, according to C. K. Barrett, often multivalent in character: a scriptural citation is intended to link up with a number of Old Testament passages; or, if no citation is actually given, a thematic relationship exists between the Johannine subject matter and episodes in the Old Testament.[4] There is a reason for this interpretive strategy. John draws a connection between Jesus as the Word and the words of the Mosaic writings: "For had ye [the Jews] believed Moses, ye would have believed me: for he wrote of me. But if ye believe not his writings, how shall ye believe my words?" (Jn 5:46, 47). In various parts of the Gospel John presents Jesus as the living embodiment of these words. The view underlying this presentation of Jesus is presumably that, again, the Word that spoke at the creation of the world continued to be active in the world that is depicted by Scripture. This view would also encourage us to be alert to the possibility that John intends to present Jesus as functioning as the Word in his own historical life too, not just in the prior world of Old Testament events and developments.

There is some evidence that Matthew opens his Gospel, especially in his phrase *biblos geneseos,* by recalling the Book of Genesis.[5] In particular, Matthew in his eschatological scheme

4. See C. K. Barrett, *The Gospel According to St. John* (London, 1955), 24, 25. When Matthew, never Mark, writes, "that which is said" or "it has been said" and does not cite the source, he is in fact citing the Pentateuch. See David Daube, *Appeasement or Resistance, and Other Essays on New Testament Judaism* (Berkeley, 1987), 8 n. 11.

5. For the various arguments in support of the thesis and the scholarly literature on it, see W. D. Davies and D. C. Allison, *The Gospel According to Saint Matthew,* ICC (Edinburgh, 1988), 1:149–60). The pronouncement of Jesus that he is Lord of the sabbath (Mt 12:8; Mk 2:28; Lk 6:5) is an equally interesting text.

is intent on presenting Jesus as bringing about a new creation. John's interpretation of the words of creation in Genesis may have this allusive, thematic character. Furthermore, by connecting Jesus and Genesis, John would be developing, not necessarily dependent on Matthew's example, some embryonic scheme that might underlie Matthew's use of the Book of Genesis.

Third, some scholars have argued that the seven days of creation in Genesis are reproduced in a Johannine scheme.[6] The feature that engages their attention is the sequence of days referred to in Jn 1:29 through 2:1. Although there are some difficulties in establishing an actual sequence of seven days—they have to appeal to inferior manuscripts—their observation does not go far enough. It is in fact this particular observation that inspired me to look at the matter from another angle.

To understand a New Testament author's use of the Hebrew or Greek Bible it is vitally important to acquire his perspective. It goes without saying that his interpretive strategy is different from ours. Moreover, just as it is difficult to give a clear and coherent account of a modern scholar's approach to Scripture and to distinguish his or hers from a contemporary's, so the same difficulty is found in differentiating, for example, John's approach from Paul's or Matthew's or, the one closest to John's, Philo's.

I concur with C. H. Dodd's view: "The author of the Fourth Gospel also had Genesis before him, and the cast of his thought clearly suggests that he was acquainted, if not with Philo, at least with Jewish thought proceeding on similar lines."[7] The point always to be borne in mind is that even if

---

6. M.-E. Boismard, *Du Baptême à Cana* (Paris, 1956), first suggested the seven-day scheme and his suggestion has met with approval, e.g., R. E. Brown, *The Gospel According to John I–XII* (New York, 1966), 105, 106; Thomas Barosse, "The Seven Days of the New Creation in St. John's Gospel," *CBQ* 21 (1959), 507–16.

7. See C. H. Dodd, *The Interpretation of the Fourth Gospel* (Cambridge, Eng., 1965), 41. "John did not depend upon Philo, but was a parallel phenomenon." So Peder Borgen, *Bread from Heaven: An Exegetical Study of the Concept of Manna in*

John's perspective differs from Philo's, the latter's is nonetheless far more helpful in understanding John's use of the Hebrew or Greek Bible than is our looking back and forth between John and any biblical text he may have used. David Daube states, "Now whenever people base on an ancient text, for a comprehension of their drift it matters little what that text means or, to put it more humbly, what we suppose it to mean; the key lies in what it means to them, which may be quite different."[8]

Shortly before John, both Philo and Josephus reinterpret Genesis 1 for their own contemporary purposes. Philo's approach has to be seen in the light of the Middle Platonism of first-century (B.C.E.) Alexandria. Just as the interpretation of Plato's physics, especially the text of his *Timaeus*, constitutes the dominant interest of the Middle Platonists, so at this time and by way of their inspiration, Jewish authors seek to explain the origin of the world by focusing on a comprehension of the pertinent texts in the Book of Genesis.[9] Philo, for example, does not discount the plain meaning of the biblical text but seeks deeper significance: "Some merely follow the outward and obvious . . . I would not censure such persons, for perhaps the truth is with them also. Still, I would exhort them not to halt there, but to press on to allegorical interpretations and to recognise that the letter is to the oracle but as the shadow to the substance, and that the higher values therein revealed are what really and truly exist" (*De Confus.* 190; cp. *De Abr.* 18).

I shall argue that John, in an imaginative, allusive approach to the text of Genesis that is akin to Philo's approach

the Gospel of John and the Writings of Philo (Leiden, 1965), 3. Borgen's fine study is worth quoting further: "John reflects common Jewish features in his exegesis and drew on haggadic and halakhic traditions, especially from early Merkabah mysticism. . . . John mainly reflects a gnosticizing tendency in accordance with similar tendencies in the development of Merkabah."

8. Daube, *Appeasement*, 1.

9. See T. H. Tobin, *The Creation of Man: Philo and the History of Interpretation* (Washington, 1983), 18.

before him, does indeed lay out the equivalent of the seven days of creation.[10] The elements of each day in Genesis have their historical counterparts in John such that these echo in allegorical fashion the details of the creation story. In the first five chapters of his Gospel Johannine historical reporting is an allegorization of the creation story, just as Philo's interpretations of Genesis 1 are primarily allegorical.

John's scheme is an extensive one that begins with the extraordinary emphasis on negatives in the description of John the Baptist's role in relation to Jesus (Jn 1:15–42) and ends with the account of Jesus' cure of the paralytic on the sabbath (John 5). My position is the opposite of Rudolf Schnackenburg's. In a comment dismissing the possibility of a reference to the week of creation in the story of the miracle at Cana of Galilee, he states: "But the thought of creation only occurs in the prologue, where it is in any case not central."[11]

The Prologue to the Gospel sets up the scheme in that it conveys the notion of Jesus as the preexistent Word (Logos) who, acting at the original creation, enters the historical realm of existence as the Word become flesh. In his discussion of the figure of the Logos in Philo's biblical interpretations, T. H.

10. See Chapter 1 for an interesting attempt to demonstrate that the six instructions about the building of the Temple (Exod 25:1; 30:11, 17, 22, 34; 31:1), followed by a command to observe the sabbath (Exod 31:12–17), correspond to the seven days of creation; see P. J. Kearney, "Creation and Liturgy: The P Redaction of Ex 25–40," *ZAW* 89 (1977), 375–87. For example, the section about the priesthood of Aaron that opens with the "light" kindled by Aaron and concludes with the "lamp" (Exod 27:20–30:10) corresponds to the creation of light in Gen 1:1–5. For Moshe Weinfeld's skepticism about such a particular type of correspondence but his support for an intimate link between creation and the Temple, see "Sabbath, Temple and the Enthronement of the Lord— The Problem of the Sitz im Leben of Genesis 1:1–2:3," *Festschrift Cazelles, AOAT* 212 (1981), 502 n. 5.

11. See Rudolf Schnackenburg, *The Gospel According to St John* (New York, 1968), 1:325. R. Alan Culpepper is one scholar alert to a broader perspective: "The gospel narrative therefore portrays Jesus as the one who continued the creative work of the divine *logos* by creating eyes for a man born blind, restoring the dead to life, and breathing spirit into spiritless disciples" (*The Anatomy of the Fourth Gospel* [Philadelphia, 1983], 34, cp. 58, 106, 107).

Tobin notes that for Philo, "The *logos* was both the power through which the universe was originally ordered and the power by which the universe continued to be ordered."[12] So too for John is the activity of Jesus during his lifetime, in effect the power of the Logos, the remedy for the imperfections that have somehow been introduced into the created order. The activity is the power to re-create. The view that the original creation in Genesis 1 was flawed already shows up in the story of the flood in Genesis 6–9.[13]

According to David Runia, Philo is interested in "a deliberate recapitulation of certain aspects of the creational sequence."[14] So too is John. John speaks of Jesus manifesting his glory (Jn 2:11). This has a precise meaning. It is the recovery of the glory he possessed with the Father before the creation of the world (Jn 17:5, 24).[15] The probably contemporary ideas about creation and re-creation in 2 Esd 6:58, 59 echo comparable concerns, if in a much less fully developed form, to those expressed in John. Israel is God's firstborn, only begotten, and the world has been created for the members of this nation. The seer, however, laments, "Why do we not possess our world as an inheritance? How long will this be so?" This section of 2 Esdras is based on Genesis 1 in that there are six days of creation and the work of each day resembles what is described in Genesis 1.

The Wisdom of Solomon (probably a first-century B.C.E. com-

12. T. H. Tobin, "Creation in Philo of Alexandria," in *Creation in the Biblical Traditions*, ed. Clifford and Collins, 116.

13. Cp. the idea as expressed in the Qumran literature: "Before they were established, he knew their works and abhorred the generations" (*CD* 2:8). On the lack of reference to the creation as good in 4 Ezra (2 Esdras) and the implications, see Joan E. Cook, "Creation in 4 Ezra: The Biblical Theme in Support of Theodicy," in *Creation in the Biblical Traditions*, ed. Clifford and Collins, 129–39.

14. David T. Runia, *Philo of Alexandria and the Timaeus of Plato* (Leiden, 1986), 554, e.g., *Ques Gen* 2.51. Runia also states, "Philo does not believe in a temporal creation but rather in a *creatio aeterna*. The cosmos is eternally being produced by the processes of God's thought" (24).

15. Schnackenburg, *St John*, 1:335–37, 555. I noted in Chapter 1 that the term "glory" had close links with the creation.

position from Alexandria in Egypt and certainly predating the Fourth Gospel)[16] provides an equally interesting use of the creation story. In his impressive commentary, David Winston shows how the author interprets the miracle of the Israelites' crossing of the Red Sea at the time of the exodus from Egypt as a refashioning of the created world of Genesis 1 (Wis 19:6–8).[17] Here then is a Hellenistic author who shares many ideas with Philo,[18] who lives before John, and who uses the creation story to interpret the history of the exodus as a new creation. This is precisely what the author of the Fourth Gospel does. John uses Genesis 1, in a much more detailed way than the author of the Wisdom of Solomon, to interpret the historical life of Jesus as bringing about a new creation. As Michael Kolarcik puts it, "By means of the personified figure of wisdom, the author [of the Wisdom of Solomon] joins together God's original creation to the continuous recreation of God in salvation history."[19] The history of the exodus and, I shall argue, the history of Jesus are viewed from the perspective of creation.[20]

16. Throughout my discussion I shall, in support of my arguments, make reference to Talmudic sources that come from a time later than the Fourth Gospel. Raymond E. Brown is a good example of a New Testament scholar who to all intents and purposes objects to such use of material because of the time difference. In the *Death of the Messiah* (New York, 1994), 1:123, in commenting on the use of the Mishnah for the illumination of New Testament ideas and practices, he rejects it as a safe guide for matters 150 years earlier in Jesus' time. He shows no recognition of the fact that often a rabbinic view, for example, about Pharaoh consulting his astrologers, that comes only from the second half of the third century C.E. (*Exod. Rabba* on 1:22), is nonetheless found in Josephus (*Ant.* 2.9.2.205), that is, in New Testament times. More often than not, scholars take the difference in time between the New Testament and the later rabbinic documents as in effect rendering the latter of no account in the study of the New Testament. Certainly such sources must be used with caution. Brown would presumably also more or less reject what Romanists have done for generation after generation in working out the history of Roman Law. They use Justinian's *Digest* of 533 C.E. as a fundamental source for Roman law of the period between 15 B.C.E. through 235 C.E..

17. David Winston, *The Wisdom of Solomon*, AB (New York, 1979), 9, 325.

18. See ibid., 59–63.

19. Michael Kolarcik, "Creation and Salvation in the Book of Wisdom," in *Creation in the Biblical Traditions*, ed. Clifford and Collins, 102.

20. See Chapter 1 for the long tradition of interpretation that links the exodus story to the creation story.

Apocalyptic works interpret history or its end as a series of seven great days or weeks, for example, the Apocalypses of Abraham 17–19 and 2 Enoch 33. John's imaginative reapplication of the seven days of creation is another example. As Dale Allison reminded me when he kindly read my manuscript, to view the history of Jesus from the perspective of creation is not in the least surprising because the heart of eschatology is that the latter things are as the first (Barn. 6:13). It is a view that is found throughout early Christian literature.[21]

I shall not pursue the issue of the historical background that produced John's Gospel. In the light of the enormous interest in cosmology in the first and second centuries of the Christian era his use of the creation story should occasion no surprise. I leave open the question whether, bearing in mind that there is a class of scribes in the first century who are much more involved in esoteric knowledge than has been recognized to date,[22] John may fit into this category. Only in a private setting with an intimate circle of students does this type of scribe discuss and explore such topics as the secrets and marvels of creation.[23] John's resort to an allegorical mode of interpretation is consistent with this setting. The original meaning of the word *allegoria* is "the other utterance in public"—different from the real one in private.[24] The outsider hears one meaning, but only the insider comprehends the deeper significance.

21. See N. A. Dahl, *Jesus in the Memory of the Early Church* (Minneapolis, 1976), 120–40. In the second century C.E. Victorinus of Pettau linked aspects of the gospels with the days of creation. See Victorinus of Pettau 3, CSEL 49 (1916), ed. Johannes Haussleiter.

22. Joachim Jeremias, *Jerusalem in the Time of Jesus* (Philadelphia, 1969), 237–39.

23. A major part of John's Gospel is the farewell speech of the master to his disciples (Jn 14–17). In ancient literature, for example, Babylonian, Egyptian, Hebrew Bible, this literary convention constitutes a classic example of a wisdom setting.

24. See David Daube, *Ancient Hebrew Fables* (Oxford, 1973), 8; also entry, "Allegorie," in *Lexicon für Theologie und Kirche* (Freiburg, 1957), 1: 346–47.

Chapter 3

Day One

(Gen 1:1–5) ¹In the beginning God created the heaven and the earth. ²And the earth was without form, and void; and darkness was upon the face of the deep. And the Spirit of God moved upon the face of the waters.

³And God said, Let there be light: and there was light. ⁴And God saw the light, that it was good: and God divided the light from the darkness. ⁵And God called the light Day, and the darkness he called Night. And the evening and the morning were the first day.

(Jn 1:15–42) ¹⁵John bare witness of him, and cried, saying, This was he of whom I spake, He that cometh after me is preferred before me; for he was before me. ¹⁶And of his fulness have all we received, and grace for grace. ¹⁷For the law was given by Moses, but grace and truth came by Jesus Christ. ¹⁸No man hath seen God at any time; the only begotten Son, which is in the bosom of the Father, he hath declared him. ¹⁹And this is the record of John, when the Jews sent priests and Levites from Jerusalem to ask him, Who art thou? ²⁰And he confessed, and denied not; but confessed, I am not the Christ. ²¹And they asked him, what then? Art thou Elias? And he saith, I am not. Art thou that Prophet? And he answered, No. ²²Then said they unto him, Who art thou? that we may give an answer to them that sent us. What sayest thou of thyself? ²³He said, I am the voice of one crying in the wilderness, Make straight the way of the Lord, as said the prophet Esaias. ²⁴And they which were sent were of the Pharisees. ²⁵And they asked him, and said unto him, Why baptizest thou then, if thou be not that

Christ, nor Elias, neither that Prophet? [26]John answered them, saying, I baptize with water: but there standeth one among you, whom ye know not; [27]He it is, who coming after me is preferred before me, whose shoe's latchet I am not worthy to unloose. [28]These things were done in Bethabara beyond Jordan, where John was baptizing.

[29]The next day John seeth Jesus coming unto him, and saith, Behold the Lamb of God, which taketh away the sin of the world! [30]This is he of whom I said, After me cometh a man which is preferred before me; for he was before me. [31]And I knew him not: but that he should be made manifest to Israel, therefore am I come baptizing with water. [32]And John bare record, saying, I saw the Spirit descending from heaven like a dove, and it abode upon him. [33]And I knew him not: but he that sent me to baptize with water, the same said unto me, Upon whom thou shalt see the Spirit descending, and remaining on him, the same is he which baptizeth with the Holy Ghost. [34]And I saw, and bare record that this is the Son of God.

[35]Again the next day after, John stood, and two of his disciples; [36]And looking upon Jesus as he walked, he saith, Behold the Lamb of God! [37]And the two disciples heard him speak, and they followed Jesus. [38]Then Jesus turned, and saw them following, and saith unto them, What seek ye? They said unto him, Rabbi, (which is to say, being interpreted, Master,) where dwellest thou? [39]He saith unto them, Come and see. They came and saw where he dwelt, and abode with him that day: for it was about the tenth hour. [40]One of the two which heard John speak, and followed him, was Andrew, Simon Peter's brother. [41]He first findeth his own brother Simon, and saith unto him, We have found the Messias, which is, being interpreted, the Christ. [42]And he brought him to Jesus. And when Jesus beheld him, he said, Thou art Simon the son of Jona: thou shalt be called Cephas, which is by interpretation, A stone.

John's description of the first meeting ever between the Baptist and Jesus contains five odd features. I shall focus on these problematic elements to communicate the thesis that John's allegorical reading of Genesis 1 is the key to a comprehension of the presentation of Jesus' life story, up to and including his healing of a man on the sabbath day (John 5). An obvious point might first be made. Genesis 1 is about beginnings. So too is John's opening account of the history of Jesus. But this is true not just in the sense of a beginning. Unlike both Matthew's and Luke's accounts, it is about the beginnings of Jesus' life in the world, namely, the public encounter between him and the Baptist.

The first problem is the much commented upon contrast between the Synoptic Gospels' depiction of the Baptist and John's depiction of him. In the Synoptics the Baptist has a positive role: he is Elijah, the forerunner of the Christ (Mk 9:13; Mt 11:14; 17:12; cp. Lk 1:17). But in John's Gospel the Baptist is defined by negative description only. He is not the Christ; he is not Elijah; he is not the Prophet (cp. Deut 18:15, 18). He is only a voice in the wilderness who speaks in the name of the prophet Isaiah, "Make straight the way of the Lord" (Isa 40:3). To informed readers this statement would be a stimulus to think about the topic of new creation. The quotation belongs to and leads off a section of the prophecy which is permeated by multiple themes of creation and renewal (e.g., Isa 40:12–31).

I account for the difference in the respective depictions of the Baptist by assuming John's dependence upon the account of creation in Genesis. Just as Jesus personifies the spoken Word of God at creation, as spelled out in the Prologue to the Gospel, so, I suggest, the Baptist's voice, which is prior to that spoken Word in terms of what actually occurred at creation, is the personified void, a harbinger of momentous change. The personification of the natural order is widespread in sources from the period of the Second Temple, for example, 2 Esd 6:41; 1 Enoch 60:15; Jub 2:2. In his narrative John presents the Baptist's activity before he introduces Jesus. John's doing so corresponds to how matters shaped up at the beginning of creation, first the void, followed by significant developments.

When John describes the Baptist by a series of negative identities he intends that the Baptist's curiously indifferent role is an echo of the primeval state of nothing in particular. Other features of the narrative confirm this link. When the Jews ask the Baptist why, if he is none of the figures of Old Testament tradition, does he baptize, the Baptist downplays his role by the redundant remark that he baptizes with water. In John's Gospel water proves to be a richly endowed symbol, but not in this instance. Indeed, John negates the significance of the Baptist's use of water. This lack of consequence matches the state of things at the beginning of the world: after the *tohu* and *bohu* there was darkness over the water. The Baptist's statement that he does not know Jesus ("And I knew him not" [Jn 1:31]) corresponds to this darkness. Only with the activity of the Spirit on the water at creation does a meaningful development take place—as is true for the Spirit at the forthcoming water baptism of Jesus, which is when the Baptist does come to know Jesus.[1]

The events that are associated with the Baptist's use of water also recall the events that are associated with the waters of the first day of creation.[2] When Jesus comes to the water to be baptized the Baptist compares the descent of the Spirit upon Jesus at that moment to a dove's flight. The comparison is the same one used in the Dead Sea Scrolls and in rabbinic exegesis about the role of the Spirit on the first day of creation: "The Spirit of God was borne over the water, as a dove which broods

1. In the Synoptic account about the Baptist his call for repentance is central. The rabbis argue that Gen 1:2, the Spirit's moving upon the waters, refers to repentance (*Gen. Rabba* 2:5). They liken repentance to water and cite Lam 2:19 ("Pour out thine heart like water") in support of their view. See Hugo Odeberg's comments, *The Fourth Gospel, Interpreted in Its Relation to Contemporaneous Religious Currents in Palestine and the Hellenistic-Oriental World* (Uppsala, 1929), 53, 54. The link between repentance and the primeval waters of day one is early, as the Coptic gnostic writing, the Apocryphon of John, reveals; see Kurt Rudolph, *Gnosis: The Nature and History of Gnosticism* (New York, 1987), 80.

2. In Mandaean sources a link is drawn between the waters of the Jordan (where John baptizes) and the water of the chaos of Gen 1:2; see Odeberg, *Fourth Gospel*, 58, 61. Patristic texts similarly associate baptism with the primitive waters of Gen 1:2; see D. C. Allison, *The New Moses: A Matthean Typology* (Minneapolis, 1993), 200.

over her young" (*b. Hag.* 15a, *y. Hag.* 77b).[3] The comparison
of the Spirit to a bird comes from the use of the word "to
hover" (*epephereto* in the Septuagint, *rhp* in the Hebrew Bible)
in the description of how the Spirit moves over the waters in
Gen 1:2. The verb describes the action of a bird hovering over
its brood.[4]

The detailed correspondences between John's account of
events and the text in Genesis are remarkable. Allegorically,
the Baptist's voice in the wilderness is the equivalent of the
tohu and *bohu*, the formlessness and void that characterize the
stage in the earth's existence before the Spirit was active.[5] Speculation about creation in sources roughly contemporaneous
with John may have claimed that there were two stages of development associated with the void of day one. In 2 Esd 6:39,
"The Spirit was hovering, and darkness and silence embraced
everything; the sound of man's voice was not yet there." The
Poimandres ("Shepherd of Men")—a first- or second-century
C.E. Hellenistic religious work from the Hermetic *Corpus* that
contains both a doctrine of the cosmic logos recalling that of
Philo and ideas decidedly reminiscent of John—may describe
the next stage: "The darkness changing into a sort of moist
nature, unspeakably agitated, giving out smoke as from a fire,
and producing a sort of ineffable, clamorous noise; and then
a cry was sent out from it inarticulately."[6] Possibly the Baptist's

3. For the link between the Spirit at creation and a dove in a recent fragment
from the Dead Sea Scrolls, see D. C. Allison, "The Baptism of Jesus and a New
Dead Sea Scroll," *BAR* 18 (1992), 58–60.

4. B. F. Westcott, *The Gospel According to St. John* (London, 1908), 21; also Odeberg, *Fourth Gospel*, 53. The Hebrew word *rhp* in Gen 1:2 occurs elsewhere only
in Deut 32:11 where the reference is to an eagle's flight. See my discussion in
Chapter 1. On the difficulty of deciding whether John uses a Hebrew text or the
Septuagint, see E. D. Freed, *Old Testament Quotations in the Gospel of John*, NTSuppl.
11 (Leiden, 1965).

5. Philo assigned the *tohu* and *bohu* to the incorporeal realm of ideas, *De Opic*
29, 32–35.

6. C. H. Dodd's translation, *The Interpretation of the Fourth Gospel* (Cambridge,
Eng., 1965), 37; and see Jörg Büchli, *Der Poimandres. Ein paganisiertes Evangelium.*

voice in the wilderness is to be thought of along the lines of this cry that proceeds from the chaos.

In any event, there must have been an audience to hear the Baptist's voice, but curiously John draws no attention whatever to it, unlike the Synoptics: "And there went out unto him all the land of Judea, and they of Jerusalem" (Mk 1:5). Why is there this pronounced difference between John and the Synoptics? At creation, although there was spoken language, there was no human audience to hear it, which must have encouraged speculation about—indeed the allegorization of—the special nature of this language.

In contrast also to the Synoptic accounts (Mk 1:11; Mt 3:17; Lk 3:22), John has no voice from heaven accompanying the descent of the Spirit. The omission may be owing to the depiction of what took place on day one at creation: there was no divine communication before the separation of the light from the darkness.

The Baptist explains that he baptizes with water so that Jesus might be revealed to Israel. For this statement to have meaning the revelatory medium of Scripture is surely the key, in this instance, I suggest, the opening of the creation story in Genesis 1. It is, moreover, revelation, not so much through the citation of Scripture but through a particular way of understanding it that John has already laid out in his Prologue. At the baptism of Jesus the Baptist bears witness that Jesus is the Son of God. We recall from the Prologue that the Baptist "who was not that light"—rather, as noted, he represents the activity that preceded the significant developments of creation—bears witness to the light, and that light is the Son of the Father (Jn 1:7, 8, 14). This is the light that shines in the darkness, the true light that "lighteth every man that cometh into the world" (Jn 1:9). For John the light that is Jesus is the light that appears on day one at the

Sprachliche und begriffliche Untersuchungen zum I. Traktat des Corpus Hermeticum, Wissenschaftliche Untersuchungen zum NT, 2 Reihe 27 (Tübingen, 1987).

creation of the world. The Prologue goes on to state, "The world was made by him" (Jn 1:10).

For John the phenomenon of the light in Genesis is, to put it in Platonic terms, a symbol or reflection of an eternal reality.[7] The important point is that John is basing his description of the Baptist in relation to Jesus upon the text about the first day of creation. In Johannine terms, Jesus as the Word who acted at creation is active again. Not only does he, as the Word, create, but his light *is* the light that appeared at the creation. Jesus in his role of replicating creation constitutes the revelation that the Baptist refers to.

The references to creation in John are not just allusive. The repeated notice in John (for example, Jn 1:15, 30) that Jesus belongs before the Baptist plainly conveys the notion that Jesus is preexistent. By this idea John indicates that the preexistence of Jesus extends back, not just to the time of creation but before that time. Jesus is the spoken language of the creation story, the Word, and since this language did not come into play just at the beginning of creation it must have been part of the divine order of things before the time of the actual creation.

I turn to the second odd feature of John's initial account of the lives of the Baptist and Jesus. Those who come to question the Baptist in the wilderness are no less than priests and Levites. They come from Jerusalem to make inquiry of the Baptist's activity. They represent the existing Temple service (Jn 1:19).[8] What is the significance of their role, which has no parallel in the Synoptics (Mt 3:1–6; Mk 1:2–6; Lk 3:1–6)? Before taking up this question it is worth turning to the third odd feature of John's narration of events.

7. In *Gen. Rabba* 3:4 God at the creation of the world wrapped himself in a white garment (Ps 104:2), in the manner of a Greek philosopher, and became in his glory the light of the world. A major feature of John is that Jesus is depicted as a wise counselor giving instruction to his disciples.

8. They are sent by the Pharisees (Jn 1:24). This information rightly causes some skepticism; see Rudolf Schnackenburg, *The Gospel According to St John* (New York, 1968), 1:292. Curiously, Schnackenburg thinks, without giving any reason, that they come from the Sanhedrin, "the central authority of the Jews" (286).

This third feature is the Baptist's words spoken on the first occasion when he actually comes into contact with Jesus. In communicating to an audience about the person coming toward them, whom neither he nor that audience has met before, the Baptist speaks in a decidedly strange way. He says, "Behold the Lamb of God, which taketh away the sin of the world" (Jn 1:29). His statement is obviously intended to suggest some profound significance. But to what does it refer? Commentators, not surprisingly, have had much difficulty with it.

In his masterly discussion of the various proposals put forward for the meaning of the reference to the Lamb of God, C. H. Dodd argues persuasively against a number of widely held views (although he is reluctant to exclude them entirely) and links the expression to a tradition shared by the Apocalypse of John (Revelation). Dodd concludes that the idea of the Lamb symbolizes the Messiah as leader of the flock of God, that is, as "King of Israel."[9] In Rev 17:14 the Lamb is called the Lord of Lords and the King of Kings. In Rev 19:16 this double title is applied to the rider of the white horse, who is also called the "Word of God" (Rev 19:13). The Word's interference in the created order leads to the renewal of the creation (Rev 21:1–22:5).

Whatever the nature of the links between the Fourth Gospel and the Book of Revelation,[10] if Dodd is correct to make this particular connection, I propose to take it further and point out that in the Apocalypse the Lamb together with God constitutes the new Temple. Moreover, the Lamb provides its light. In his vision of the new Jerusalem the seer John states, "And I saw no temple therein: for the Lord God Almighty and the Lamb are the temple of it. And the city had no need of the

9. Dodd, *Interpretation*, 236; for his discussion, see 230–38. In Rev 7:17 the Lamb is the shepherd.

10. Freedom of attribution in the Fourth Gospel, where words are freely attributed to Jesus, and a similar freedom in Revelation should not conceal essential similarities between the two works. Early Christian writers assumed that the one author John wrote both books.

sun, neither of the moon, to shine in it: for the glory of God did lighten it, and the Lamb is the light thereof" (Rev 21:22, 23). The evangelist John has already made allusion to the Temple, precisely in regard to Jesus' "residence": "And the Word became flesh and tabernacled among us" (Jn 1:14).[11] The implication is that Jesus makes the Word flesh in his capacity as the new Temple, an identification that is made explicit in Jn 2:21 ("But he [Jesus] spake of the temple of his body").

If we can assume this background of meaning about the new Temple, so much is made clearer when we look at the context in which the Baptist refers to Jesus as the Lamb of God that takes away the sins of the world. We might first note that the lamb as a sacrificial animal was very much associated with the Temple service; for example, there was the perpetual sacrifice of a lamb in the Temple, the *tamid*, the offering each morning and evening of a lamb without blemish (Exod 29:38; Num 28:3; Ezek 46:13; Dn 8:11, 12, 13; 11:31; 12:11). Second, in 1 Peter 1:19, 20, Jesus is identified as the unblemished, sacrificial lamb whose purpose "was foreordained before the foundation of the world."

Third, and most important, the priests and the Levites who come from Jerusalem to make inquiry of the Baptist's activity represent the existing Temple service. The Baptist's statement about Jesus as the Lamb is indeed the disclosure that is the answer to their inquiry about the Baptist's role. Although we are not told explicitly to whom the Baptist makes his statement, it is nonetheless clear that we are to understand the audience to include those who represent the Temple service, namely, the priests and the Levites.

John makes no explicit mention of the Temple. This omission may itself be significant. The idea of a new heavenly Temple, while owing something to the influence of Plato's philosophy on Hellenistic Judaism before 70 C.E., must have been stimulated by the destruction of the Jerusalem Temple in

---

11. See R. E. Brown, *The Gospel According to John I–XII*, AB (New York, 1966), 32–34.

that year. John writes at a time when the priests and Levites have lost their old identity yet were surely seeking to redefine it without reference to the ruined Temple.[12] John's account about their inquiry could therefore reflect his contemporary reality. In characteristically allusive fashion, with the reference to Jesus as the Lamb of God that takes away the sins of the world, he switches from the manifest ruins of the Temple service—truly symbolic of the sins of the world—to Jesus as the light of the New Temple, hence of the renewed creation that is freed from imperfection. The link between the Temple and the creation of the world is indeed an important one and it pervades John's presentation of the Baptist's activity.

Rabbinic thought provides parallels to Johannine and supports the importance of this link between the Temple and creation. In Jub 1:27, 28, a direct link is drawn between the work of creation and the aim of establishing an eternal Temple. Like Jesus for John, the Temple precedes the creation of the world, and light is created from the place of the Temple (*Gen. Rabba* 1:4). The world is not really created until man does God's will by erecting the Temple. Once the Temple is erected, God's original intention to be one with man is fulfilled (*Gen. Rabba* 1:9). Like John, the rabbis speak not about the past but about the present, a present in which the physical Temple no longer exists.

The fourth problematic element in John's account of the beginnings of Jesus' public life is the notice about how two of the Baptist's disciples go to Jesus' own home and "abode with him that day for it was about the tenth hour" (Jn 1:39). They end up there because the Baptist says to them at the approach of Jesus, "Behold the Lamb of God" (Jn 1:36). The exact sig-

---

12. On the issue of replacing the Temple service after 70 C.E., see W. D. Davies, *The Setting of the Sermon on the Mount* (Atlanta, 1989), 256–72. Once when Rabbi Akiba and his friends came upon the desecrated ruins of the Temple, they wept but he laughed. Explaining his odd reaction, Akiba stated that as God had fulfilled the prophecies of destruction, so they could be assured that he would fulfill those of restoration, *b. Mak.* 24b. The contrast between the old Temple and a new one is comparable to John's stance. The two views are also close in time.

nificance of this reference to the day in John has proved elusive. The time mentioned in some manuscripts is the tenth hour: four in the afternoon if, as most commentators believe, the Jewish method of enumerating time (from dawn to dark) applies.[13] The problem is then to understand why there is the reference to "that day." Rudolf Schnackenburg wonders if the day that follows the evening is also included. He would be right if the days of creation are in John's mind because "there was evening and there was morning, one day" (Gen 1:5).[14]

In discussing the symbolic use of time in the Fourth Gospel, J. E. Bruns argues in favor of the reading, "It was about the sixth hour," in the Codex Alexandrinus. The reference then is to high noon, the hour of greatest light from the sun, and signifies the notion of Jesus as the light of the world.[15] "That day" in Jn 1:39 would then allude to the light that shines by day, reminiscent of the light that is called day in Gen 1:5, or, alternatively, that rules the day according to Gen 1:16.[16] Both readings would make sense if we can assume similar interests in the allegorical explication of the days of creation by the writer of the Gospel and a later transmitter of it.

The appearance of light is the dominant feature of the first day of creation. Not surprisingly, the notion of Jesus as the light correspondingly dominates John's presentation at this point in his Gospel. The Baptist, whose role is to bear witness to the light (Jn 1:8), turns two of his disciples to it when he declares to them that Jesus is the Lamb of God. When the Baptist refers to his own ignorance ("and I knew him not") the contrast is

13. For counterarguments that the Roman system applies, see R. Alan Culpepper, *The Anatomy of the Fourth Gospel* (Philadelphia, 1983), 219.

14. Schnackenburg, *St John*, 309. *m. Hull.* 5:5 speaks of how one day in the story of creation is daytime together with the night that went before.

15. J. E. Bruns, "The Use of Time in the Fourth Gospel," *NTS* 13 (1966), 285–90.

16. The relationship between the light that came into existence at God's command on day one and the light that came from the sun on day three was a productive source of speculation in Judaism. In distinguishing the one from the other, the rabbis (for example, in *Gen. Rabba* 3:6) readily allegorized the light of the first day as that which was stored for the righteous in the Messianic future.

between darkness and light, again reminiscent of day one of creation.

When the disciples ask Jesus where he dwells he invites them to come and see. This they do, and they stay with him "that day." We recall that in the Prologue Jesus as the true light comes to his own home, but his own do not receive him (Jn 1:11). Here those who come to his home and seek the true light, the Lamb that takes away the sins of the world and is the light of the new Temple, are received by him in his own home. In Jn 9:4 (cp. 8:12) the notion of seeing in the sense of the enlightenment that typically a disciple might seek from a master is associated with the daytime. That the two disciples stay with Jesus "that day" is indeed a suggestive link with the creation story, although we must remember that for John, as for Philo, the days of creation are not to be equated with the ordinary days of the week. It is no surprise, however, that a symbolic link exists between them.

The fifth and final puzzle is why Jesus gives Simon the name Peter, the "Rock," as soon as they meet and not, as in Matthew (Mt 16:17, 18), much later into their life together. John's absorption with the theme of creation can illumine why this naming of Simon as Peter in the Fourth Gospel stands in contrast to what Matthew does. The Baptist and Jesus, if not actually named the void and the light respectively, are identified with these two entities of day one of creation. The act of naming Peter the Rock possibly recalls the comparable act of naming the various entities, the light, the darkness, the firmament, the dry land, and so on in the Genesis creation story itself.

However that may be, a later commentary on Genesis (*Gen. Rabba* 1:4) has it that the patriarchs of Israel were contemplated before the creation of the world. This idea is around in New Testament circles because the Book of Revelation has a similar notion. As in other apocalyptic works (2 Esd 7:30, Barn. 6:13), the meaning that these authors seek to attribute to the end of time they derive from reflections about the beginning of time. The wall of the new Jerusalem has twelve foundations and on them the twelve names of the twelve apostles of the

Lamb (Rev 21:14). Peter is one of these foundations. In naming him the Rock, Jesus in John's Gospel may be pointing to
Peter's status as determined at the creation of the world. In
both Jewish literature before and after New Testament times,
the rock at the base of the Temple is the center of the world,
sealing off the abysses below.[17]

According to rabbinic tradition, God found a rock (*petra*),
Abraham, on which to build and establish the world (*Yalkuth
to Num* 23:9). Given the enormous interest in cosmology before the composition of the Fourth Gospel, for example, in
Philo, this view (if not the text in question) is just as likely to
predate Christian interpretation than to be a counteracting
claim against the Christian position on the part of the rabbis.[18]
In biblical tradition the prophet Isaiah expresses the notion
that an Israelite looks to Abraham as he looks to God as the
Rock "whence ye are hewn" (Isa 51:1, 2). Simon Peter as the
Rock may fit into John's scheme of new creation because John
shares the vision of the new world's foundations in Rev 21:14.
In 2 Bar 57:2—a Jewish work more or less contemporary with
John and designed to give hope to Jews in Palestine and in the
Diaspora after the destruction of the Temple—the advent of
Abraham signifies: "Hope for a world to be renewed was then
established; and the promise of a life to come hereafter was
implanted in men's hearts," cp. *LAB* (Pseudo-Philo) 4.11.

Rudolf Schnackenburg argues that the disciples correspond
to the original patriarchs, the founders of the nation Israel. He

17. See Peter Hayman, who cites ample evidence that the Temple was a cosmic
symbol before New Testament times, "Some Observations on *Sefer Yesira*: (2) The
Temple at the Centre of the Universe," *JJS* 37 (1986), 178. See also W. D. Davies
and D. C. Allison, *Gospel According to Saint Matthew*, ICC (Edinburgh, 1991), 2:
627, 628.

18. Moreover, the Matthean notion of Peter as a foundation of the new church
(cp. Ephes 2:20) is more likely to be derived from some existing notion in Matthew's Jewish background than to be an original idea of his. A similar consideration applies to the Johannine notion. Even if the rabbinic assertion about
Abraham is a reaction to the Christian one about Peter, we should still learn
something from the particular way in which the rabbis chose to counter the
Christian claim.

notes that the evangelist John presents the testimony of the Baptist according to a clear plan: "First he [the Baptist] acts as a witness (cp. 1:6–8) before official Judaism (the envoys from Jerusalem 1:19–28), in a rather indirect and negative way; then before 'Israel', the people of God, in a positive way (1:29–34)."[19] When Jesus acquires his first disciples through the Baptist, these disciples, Schnackenburg suggests, represent the true Israel, a name that he notes is used only in a positive sense in the Fourth Gospel. What Schnackenburg fails to see is that the election of Israel is tied up with the idea of creation. The roughly contemporary apocalyptic work 2 Esdras (4 Ezra), for example, juxtaposes the theme of creation and the election of Israel. Rabbinic sources (for example, *b. Ber.* 32b; *Gen. Rabba* 12:2) well document the notion that creation was for the sake of Israel.[20] Schnackenburg does point out that both at Qumran and in early pre-Christian Jewish thought there is the notion of how the twelve tribes of Israel will come together at some future glorious temple.[21] His observation supports my claim that the evangelist sets down his material at this point in his Gospel with the notion that the new Temple will play an important role. John thinks of the new, or true, Temple as existing before creation, and his views about it are consequently wedded to ideas about creation.

In conclusion, the opening section of Gen 1:1–5 refers to the significance of all that is going to take place, namely, the creation of the heaven and the earth (vs. 1). The opening section of John's write-up about the Baptist's role in relation to Jesus does likewise. Thus Jn 1:15–18 affirms that the sum of all that is about to develop can be expressed in the contrast between the old order and the new, between the law of Moses and the grace and truth of Jesus. John even employs the language of creation in this opening summary: the begotten son

19. Schnackenburg, *St John*, 1:285.
20. See M. E. Stone, *Fourth Ezra*, *Hermeneia*, ed. F. M. Cross (Minneapolis, 1990), 188, cp. 182.
21. Schnackenburg, *St John*, 1:285, 290 n. 20, 306.

who resides in the bosom of his father (vs. 18). From the opening summaries in each composition there follows, as I have indicated, a more or less sequence of matching developments, with John's sequence taking its cue from the sequence of events in Genesis 1.

Chapter 4

Day Two

(Gen 1:6–8) [6]And God said, Let there be a firmament in the midst of the waters, and let it divide the waters from the waters. [7]And God made the firmament, and divided the waters which were under the firmament from the waters which were above the firmament: and it was so. [8]And God called the firmament Heaven. And the evening and the morning were the second day.

(Jn 1:43–51) [43]The day following Jesus would go forth into Galilee, and findeth Philip, and saith unto him, follow me. [44]Now Philip was of Bethsaida, the city of Andrew and Peter. [45]Philip findeth Nathanael, and saith unto him, We have found him, of whom Moses in the law, and the prophets, did write, Jesus of Nazareth, the son of Joseph. [46]And Nathanael said unto him, Can there any good thing come out of Nazareth? Philip saith unto him, Come and see. [47]Jesus saw Nathanael coming to him, and saith of him, Behold an Israelite indeed, in whom is no guile! [48]Nathanael saith unto him, Whence knowest thou me? Jesus answered and said unto him, Before that Philip called thee, when thou wast under the fig tree, I saw thee. [49]Nathanael answered and saith unto him, Rabbi, thou art the Son of God; thou art the King of Israel. [50]Jesus answered and said unto him, Because I said unto thee, I saw thee under the fig tree, believest thou? thou shalt see greater things than these. [51]And he saith unto him, Verily, verily, I say unto you, Hereafter ye shall see heaven open, and the angels of God ascending and descending upon the son of man.

In John's time the belief was widespread that special knowledge, *gnosis*, resided in the heavenly realm above the firmament that came into existence on the second day of creation. For example, in 1 En 17:4, "And they [the angels] took me to the living waters," is a reference to the symbolical water above the firmament. Philo refers to the words of God that have been "poured like rain out of that lofty and pure region of life to which the prophet [Moses] has given the title of 'heaven' " (*Leg. All.* 3.163). In Justin's gnostic system, based as it is on an allegorization of the Old Testament, the initiate enters the upper world of the good and drinks the water there. This water is the water above the firmament (Gen 1:7) of the evil creation in which the *pneumatikoi* (the spiritual) wash, as distinct from the waters below the firmament in which the *psuchikoi* "men of dust and breath" wash.[1] In that ordinary human experience cannot relate to the notion that there are waters above the firmament of the created universe, it is understandable how the description of the second day of creation in Gen 1:6–8 invited symbolic meaning to be attributed to these waters. The light of day one which differed from the sunlight of day three was similarly inviting of allegorization.[2]

The relationship of the Fourth Gospel to gnostic belief is complex and receives extensive discussion. It is sufficient for my purposes to point out that some aspects of gnostic thought predate John.[3] Indeed, there is increasing recognition that an emerging *gnosis*, strongly colored with Jewish traits, deeply influenced John, and that within the Johannine community there was constant controversy in regard to gnostic interpretations about Jesus.[4] Hugo Odeberg argues that the symbolical use of

1. See C. H. Dodd, *The Interpretation of the Fourth Gospel* (Cambridge, Eng., 1965), 103–9; also 138, where he points out that Justin's interpretation is based on the Hebrew creation story.

2. See note 16, Chapter 3.

3. "Clearly, John already had an understanding of Gnosis that had undergone a process of reflection and had been adapted to Christian tradition," writes Kurt Rudolph, *Gnosis: The Nature and History of Gnosticism* (New York, 1987), 306, cp. 149.

4. See Gunter Stemberger, " 'Er Kam in sein Eigentum.' Das Johannesevan-

water in the gnostic writings is not derived from John, but
rather that it comes from mystical interpretation of the Old
Testament in John's time.[5] Even where the influence of John
on the extant gnostic literature is likely, for example, the documents representing the teaching of Basilides and Valentinus,[6]
the later gnostic writers can show us what appeared to them to
be some of John's ideas.

The enigmatic encounter between Jesus and Nathanael becomes more intelligible when we relate it to ideas associated
with what is above the firmament of day two of creation. In Jn
1:43–51, Nathanael searches, we are to learn, for knowledge
of a special kind, and there is an unmistakable emphasis on
movement from lower to higher levels of knowledge. The focus
throughout is on the higher. This focus ties in with the fact
that even a plain reading of day two of creation in Gen 1:6–8,
in which there is no explicit reference to the earth, reveals a
focus on the heavens. The one certain indication that the firmament of the second day of creation comes into play in John's
Gospel is in the climactic promise made to Nathanael by Jesus
(Jn 1:51). The heaven will have opened for Nathanael, that is,
at the firmament, and the angels—associated with the second
day of creation in some sources (e.g., 2 Esd 6:41; *Gen. Rabba*
1:3)—will ascend and descend upon Jesus, whom Nathanael
has just recognized as the Son of God, as the King of Israel.

There are two reasons why Nathanael's recognition of who
Jesus is invites the response that John has Jesus make about the
opening of the heavens. One, C. H. Dodd argues that when
John designates Jesus as the King of Israel, it is the equivalent
to his designating Jesus as the *heavenly* lamb that symbolizes the
Messiah as leader of the flock of God.[7] Two, when the Baptist

---

gelium im Dialog mit der Gnosis," *Wort und Wahrheit* 28 (1973), 435–52; cp.
Helmut Koester, "The History-of-Religions School, Gnosis, and Gospel of John,"
StTh 40 (1986), 126–32.

5. Hugo Odeberg, *The Fourth Gospel Interpreted in Its Relation to Contemporaneous
Religious Currents in Palestine and the Hellenistic-Oriental World* (Uppsala, 1929), 167.

6. See Rudolph, *Gnosis*, 17.

7. Dodd, *Interpretation*, 236.

received communication about Jesus' status as the Son of God
it comes through the descent of the Spirit from the upper firmament upon Jesus at his baptism in the lower waters of creation. Nathanael's promised initiation into heavenly mysteries
is to be understood in the same way as the Baptist's.

The knowledge that is promised to Nathanael will be of an
order different from the one he seeks when, sitting under the
fig tree, he apparently studies Scripture. In rabbinic sources a
favorite place for rabbis to study and search Scripture is sitting
under a tree.[8] In coming upon Nathanael under the fig tree,
Philip refers immediately to what Scripture revealed to Jesus'
new followers: "We have found him, of whom Moses in the
law, and the prophets, did write, Jesus of Nazareth, the son of
Joseph" (Jn 1:45). This communication to Nathanael suggests
that his preoccupation under the fig tree is indeed the study
of Scripture. If this suggestion is correct, then John may be
pointing to a specific contrast between the lower and upper
waters such as is found when the Baptist received knowledge
about Jesus as the Son of God.

The Scriptures in which Nathanael is probably immersed
constitute Torah, which rabbinic literature constantly compares to water. As C. H. Dodd points out, the contrast between
Torah and Jesus as the incarnate Word is one of the governing
ideas of the Fourth Gospel and appears in various symbolic
forms.[9] The contrast in Nathanael's situation would be between
the waters of the Torah drunk under the fig tree and the waters
above the firmament of the heavens offered to those reborn of
the Spirit. For Philo the firmament of day two was, because of
its access to heavenly knowledge of the kind that Jesus promises
Nathanael, the best part of the created world (*De Opic.* 27, 82;
Ques Gen 4.215).

Jesus' promise to Nathanael, as has long been recognized,
recalls Jacob's ladder dream of Gen 28:10–17. The ladder that

8. Hermann Strack and Paul Billerbeck, *Kommentar zum Neuen Testament aus Talmud und Midrasch* (Munich, 1924), 2:371; also 1:858.
9. Dodd, *Interpretation*, 83.

reached up to the gate of heaven, however, has been personified to mean that Jesus is the means of communication between heaven and earth.[10] John brings the text in Gen 28:12,
which does not mention the opening of the heavens, into association with the text in Gen 1:6–8. This subordination of one
text to another is widespread in Philo, the Palestinian Midrashim, and John.[11] The result in this instance is that the cosmological, gnostic speculation inspired by the text in Gen 1:6–
8 about creation prompts John to give notice of Nathanael's
future initiation into heavenly mysteries. We have an excellent
illustration of how John allegorizes a supposed historical incident in line with the creation story.

Further observations about Nathanael's progress lend support to the distinction, as understood in John's time, between
the implied lower and upper regions of day two of creation. It
is first important to point out that John elsewhere in his Gospel
works with a comparable distinction between lower and upper.
In a later episode Jesus informs Nicodemus: "If I have told you
earthly things, and ye believe not, how shall ye believe, if I tell
you heavenly things. And no man hath ascended up to heaven,
except the one out of heaven having come down, the son of
man" (Jn 3:12, 13). Jesus has been talking to Nicodemus of
the need to be born of water and the Spirit—the water and
Spirit of creation may be echoed in his remark—to enter the
kingdom of God (Jn 3:5): lower, earthly developments leading
to upper, heavenly ones. When in another episode the Pharisees take exception to Jesus' claim, one that reflects day one
of creation, that he is the light of the world and that those who
follow him will not walk in darkness (Jn 8:12), Jesus differen-

10. See R. H. Lightfoot, *St. John's Gospel* (Oxford, 1956), 104. I accept Geza
Vermes's support of Dalman's view that the term "son of man" reflects the linguistic convention in Aramaic whereby sometimes a person, for reasons of mod-
esty or awe, refers to himself in the third person ("The 'Son of Man' Debate,"
JSNT 1 [1978], 28, 29).

11. See Peder Borgen, *Bread from Heaven: An Exegetical Study of the Concept of
Manna in the Gospel of John and the Writings of Philo* (Leiden, 1965), 38–43, 52.

tiates himself from them by stating: "Ye are from beneath; I am from above: ye are of this world; I am not of this world" (Jn 8:23). We need only recall Jesus' further claim in the incident about the Samaritan woman that he is the source of everlasting water (Jn 4:14) to suggest that, like the Samaritan woman who undergoes re-creation, Nathanael can expect to drink of the water that is above the firmament.

The contrast between lower and upper emerges clearly from the pericope about Nathanael. John first depicts Jesus in lower, earthly terms as belonging to Nazareth and as the son of Joseph (Jn 1:45). From asking whether anything good can come out of a certain geographical place on the earth, Nazareth, Nathanael attains the startling knowledge that Jesus is the Son of God, the King of Israel. Nathanael attains this higher knowledge about divine sonship while under a fig tree, an even more specific designation of an earthly location. We recall that at the time of the Baptist's use of the lower waters of creation the Spirit descends from heaven, the location of the upper waters, and reveals Jesus' divine sonship (Jn 1:33, 34).

Although they have never met before, Jesus shows prescience in knowing who Nathanael is.[12] This rare kind of knowledge has an interesting parallel in the description of Enoch in extrabiblical material. In rabbinical mystical texts going back to the second century C.E., this early biblical figure came to stand for Metatron, the Celestial Being. The author of 3 En 11:1 links Enoch's prescience to the wisdom of the creator, "The Holy One, blessed be He, revealed to me [Metatron] from the beginning all the mysteries of Torah and all the secrets of Wisdom and all the depths of the Perfect Torah [Ps 19:8]; and all the thoughts of the hearts of the created [beings] and all the secrets of the universe and all the secrets of the Creation were

---

12. Compare the example of the Tannaite Gamaliel II, president of the academy at Jabneh, who identifies a person he has never met before: "He recognised him through the holy spirit and from his words we learnt three things" (*t. Pes.* 1:27; *y. A. Zar.* 40a; *b. Erub.* 64b; *Lev. Rabba* on 27:2).

revealed before me in the way in which they are revealed before the Maker of Creation" (Odeberg's translation).[13]

Equally interesting is 2 Esd 16:53–63, an apocalyptic oracle that affirms divine omniscience. In support of the view that God knows what is in man the author sets out a recital of God's creation. In doing so he especially draws attention to the manifold role of water throughout the cosmos. The recital, as Joan E. Cook points out,[14] implies a knowledgeable creator who, if he can fashion such a well-run universe, also sees into the secrets of human beings.[15] The recital is preceded by the statement: "The Lord certainly knows everything that people do; he knows their imaginations and their thoughts and their hearts" (2 Esd 16:54). It ends with a similar statement: "He knows your imaginations and what you think in your hearts!" (2 Esd 16:63). Why there is so much focus on the water in the created order to support the view of God's omniscience is not made clear in the text. The metaphor of water as knowledge may be pertinent.

A characteristic feature of John is his interplay between the literal and the figurative. In the geographical information that he gives, he may be playing with the plain sense of the waters under the firmament. Although the lower waters are primarily associated with the next day of creation, day three, it is important to point out that John, like Philo ("To each of the days He assigned some of the portions of the whole" [*De Opic.* 15]), viewed the features of the other days of creation as showing up in each of the days. John deliberately raises the issue of a place's significance, in this instance of a decidedly lower order, when he focuses attention on the place of Jesus' origin, Nazareth. Philip's place of origin is Bethsaida. It means "place of

---

13. Odeberg, *Fourth Gospel*, 43–47.

14. Joan E. Cook, "Creation in 4 Ezra: The Biblical Theme in Support of Theodicy," in *Creation in the Biblical Traditions*, ed. R. J. Clifford and J. J. Collins, CBQMS 24 (Washington, 1992), 135.

15. M. E. Stone stresses, however, that the author of 2 Esdras (4 Ezra) has reservations about the possibilities of special knowledge (*Selected Studies in Pseudepigrapha and Apocrypha* [Leiden, 1991], 385).

the fishery." The town is by the sea of Galilee, and Galilee, to which Jesus "wished to go forth" (Jn 1:43), is for those going in that direction toward the sea (Mt 4:15). Birger Olsson has called attention to the geographical symbolism associated with Galilee.[16] We might recall how on John's day one of his scheme of creation he begins its description by immediately introducing the Baptist as allegorically corresponding to the initial "nothingness" of the first day of creation in Gen 1:2. For day two of his scheme John may intend his initial information that Philip is from Bethsaida—a place by the sea—to line up allegorically with the implied waters under the firmament of Gen 1:7.

Like the rabbis, John, it would appear, links the origin of the patriarchs of the Book of Genesis to the creation story. The rabbis argue that God contemplated the creation of the patriarchs before the creation of the world (*Gen. Rabba* 1:4). To support this contention they cite Hos 9:10: "I [God] saw your fathers as the first-ripe in the fig tree at her first season." The argument appears to be as follows. The law required that the fruit of a newly planted fig tree could not be given over for common human consumption until its fifth year (Lev 19:23–25). On the basis of the view that God would adhere to his own Torah, the first fruit of the fig tree at her first season must refer to the time before the fig trees were made available for human consumption at the creation of the world (Gen 1:11). For the rabbis, then, Scripture in Hos 9:10 "proved" that God beheld the patriarchs themselves before creation.

One clue in John's text that there may be a similar way of thinking to the rabbinic one about the patriarchs and the fig tree is that both Jesus' prescient remark, "Before that Philip called thee, when thou wast under the fig tree, I saw thee," and Nathanael's response, "Rabbi, thou art the Son of God;

16. See Birger Olsson, *Structure and Meaning in the Fourth Gospel* (Lund, 1974), 27–29. Thomas L. Brodie aptly states, "While the theological dimension of John's cities is strong, their hold on history is often fragile" (*The Quest for the Origin of John's Gospel* [Oxford, 1993], 161).

thou art the King of Israel" (Jn 1:48), constitute, like Hos 9:
10 for the rabbis, coded communication. The concealed background in each instance is Scripture. The rabbis understand
the statement in Hos 9:10 (the Prophets) as commentary on
the story of creation in Genesis (the Law). In John Philip tells
Nathanael that he has discovered the person, Jesus, whom
Moses wrote about in the Law and the Prophets. Jesus, in turn,
because of his knowledge of Scripture, possibly even the text
in Hos 9:10, knows who the person studying Scripture under
the fig tree is. That person, moreover, turns out to be one of
the original patriarchs in the Book of Genesis (the Law),
namely, Jacob, whose true significance emerges only when his
ladder dream puts him in touch with heavenly mysteries associated with the firmament of the second day of creation.

How, then, is Nathanael not just one of the original patriarchs but one that was contemplated before the creation of the
world? Nathanael recognizes Jesus as the Son of God. This
status, according to John's Prologue, means that Jesus was
preexistent, "begotten of the father" (1:14). Jesus then, in his
superior insight into who Nathanael really is when he sees him
under the fig tree, is also hinting that his special knowledge
about Nathanael is precisely because Nathanael existed before
the creation of the world.

The prior meeting that Peter has with Jesus brings in the
notion, I argued, of the patriarch Abraham as *petra*, the Rock.
Nathanael's promised meeting with Jesus at the opening to the
heavens links him, as has long been recognized, to the patriarch Jacob.[17] The meeting parallels Jacob's meeting with the
angels in Gen 28:12–15. Jesus' statement about Nathanael as

17. See C. K. Barrett, *The Gospel According to St. John*, 2d ed. (Philadelphia,
1978), 185. In Jewish sources, Jacob saw the heavenly and earthly Jerusalems and
commented on the work of the Messiah (Louis Ginzberg, *The Legends of the Jews*
[Philadelphia, 1942], 3:447). Barrett points out (pp. 184–85) that the use of the
term "Israelite" in regard to Nathanael may reflect Philo's interpretation of the
name Israel (Jacob) as "seeing God" (*De Mut.* 81; *Ques Gen* 3.49, and frequently
in his writings). On the contrast between the celestial and terrestrial man in *Gen.
Rabba* 68:18 and the relevance to Jesus and the believer in him in Jn 1:51, see
Odeberg, *Fourth Gospel*, 35, 36.

an Israelite in whom there is no guile contains a contrast between the new Jacob, Nathanael, and the old Jacob. The old
Jacob in the Book of Genesis practices deception in his dealings with Esau and Laban (cp. Hos 12:1–6). By contrast, Nathanael is the ideal Israelite, the original Jacob-Israel whom
Jesus contemplated before he created the world. Probably what
also contributes to this notion of a guile-free, ideal Jacob is that
Gen 25:27 describes him as *'ish tam* ("plain man"), understood
in rabbinic times as of "plain piety." In Talmudic language
(for example, *m. B.K.* 1:4–5.) there is an antithesis between
things normally harmless (*tam*) and things likely to cause injury
(*mu' adh*). In Peter and Nathanael there emerge the true patriarchs, the ones contemplated before the creation, as in the
rabbinic notion about how God contemplated the patriarchs
before the creation of the world. The Johannine and rabbinic
speculations, each linked to the creation story, about the origin
of the patriarchs are along similar lines.

Two other pieces of evidence prove suggestive for linking the
Nathanael episode to ideas about the second day of creation.
First, in the *Poimandres*—the first- or second-century C.E. Hellenistic religious work from the Hermetic *Corpus* that has similar
ideas to both Philo and John—we learn that the man who seeks
salvation, when he ascends into the heavens, gives up evil de-
vices. The one singled out is guile (C.H. 1.24–26). The author of
the *Poimandres* bases his interpretation about the ascent from
the lower, material world into the spheres above the firmament
on the creation myth of Genesis and in particular on its description of day two. The parallel with the guile-free Nathanael, who
is assured of some comparable form of ascent into the heavenly
realm, is remarkable. The *Poimandres* is in many aspects closely
related to Johannine thought, and its interpretation of Genesis
belongs to the Jewish Hellenistic exegesis of Alexandria. Even if
the written document belongs to a period shortly after the composition of the Fourth Gospel, there can be little doubt that
John and its author are working with similar ideas.[18]

18. C. H. Dodd's work on the affinities between the Fourth Gospel and, in

Second, the angels that will be for Nathanael the means of mediating between the upper and lower waters of the firmament are associated with day two of creation.[19] According to Rabbi Johanan in *Gen. Rabba* 1:3, they were created on that day.[20] Rabbi Johanan quotes Ps 104:3 to "prove" it: "Who layest [on the second day of creation] the beams of Thine upper chambers in the waters," is followed by in verse 4, "Who makest the spirits Thine angels." In the part of 2 Esdras that predates John there is reference to the angel that, as the spirit of the firmament, divided and separated the waters on the second day of creation (2 Esd 6:41).

Unlike John's "day" one of creation in which a number of different events takes place over a number of earthly days, his second "day" has but the one event, the meeting between Jesus and Nathanael, that occurs on one earthly day. This distribution of events lines up with what we find in the pre-Johannine description of creation in Jub 2:1–18. For the author of Jubilees there were seven works on the first day but just one on the second (vv. 3, 5, cp. Philo, *De Opic.* 29).

---

particular, the *Poimandres* is indispensable. See *The Bible and the Greeks* (London, 1935), 99–209; *Interpretation*, 30–44.

19. John uses the word "angel" in only two other places, Jn 12:29, 20:12, where the idea of ascending into the heavens is again prominent.

20. According to Jub 2:2 the angels or spirits of other elements of the universe were created on the first day.

Chapter 5

Day Three

(Gen 1:9–13) [9]And God said, Let the waters under the heaven be gathered together unto one place, and let the dry land appear: and it was so. [10]And God called the dry land Earth; and the gathering together of the waters called he Seas: and God saw that it was good. [11]And God said, Let the earth bring forth grass, the herb yielding seed, and the fruit-tree yielding fruit after his kind, whose seed is in itself, upon the earth: and it was so. [12]And the earth brought forth grass, and herb yielding seed after his kind, and the tree yielding fruit, whose seed was in itself, after his kind: and God saw that it was good. [13]And the evening and the morning were the third day.

(Jn 2:1–12) [1]And the third day there was a marriage in Cana of Galilee; and the mother of Jesus was there: [2]And both Jesus was called, and his disciples, to the marriage. [3]And when they wanted wine, the mother of Jesus saith unto him, They have no wine. [4]Jesus saith unto her, Woman, what have I to do with thee? mine hour is not yet come. [5]His mother saith unto the servants, Whatsoever he saith unto you, do it. [6]And there were set there six waterpots of stone, after the manner of the purifying of the Jews, containing two or three firkins apiece. [7]Jesus saith unto them, Fill the waterpots with water. And they filled them up to the brim. [8]And he saith unto them, Draw out now, and bear unto the governor of the feast. And they bare it. [9]When the ruler of the feast had tasted the water that was made wine, and knew not whence it was, but the servants which drew the water knew, the governor of the feast called the bridegroom, [10]And saith unto him, Every man at the beginning doth set forth good wine; and when men have well drunk, then that which is worse: but thou hast kept the good wine until now.

> [11]This beginning of miracles did Jesus in Cana of Galilee, and manifested forth his glory; and his disciples believed on him.
>
> [12]After this he went down to Capernaum, he, and his mother, and his brethren, and his disciples; and they continued there not many days.

Unique to the Fourth Gospel, the miracle story of the water turned into wine has proved to be one of the most elusive to interpret. C. H. Dodd points out that on the face of it, the story appears to be a naive tale about a marvel at a village wedding.[1] He notes its realism. There is an eye for character and for seemingly trivial detail—the waterpots hold from seventeen to twenty-five gallons apiece—and there is the homely humor in the remark of the steward of the banquet: "Everyone puts the best wine on the table first, and brings on the poor stuff when the company is drunk; but you have kept your good wine to the last" (Dodd's translation). We then find the typical Johannine comment that brings out his theological interpretation of a tale: "This beginning of the signs did Jesus in Cana of Galilee, and manifested forth his glory." The verse commonly cited in comparison is Jn 1:14 about how the Word became flesh and his glory was to be beheld. The Word is the agency that spoke at creation, the uttered speech of the creation story.[2] The miracle story in John is not to be taken at its face value. Its true meaning lies deeper, but where that meaning lies has been difficult to fathom.

The usual approach of commentators is to contrast the new Christian order with the entire system of Jewish ceremonial observance.[3] The waterpots are there in accordance with the

---

1. C. H. Dodd, *The Interpretation of the Fourth Gospel* (Cambridge, Eng., 1965), 297.

2. Rudolf Schnackenburg, *The Gospel According to St John* (New York, 1968), 1: 336 n. 29, observes that the Old Testament notion of the glory of God that underlies the term *doxa* in the New Testament can refer to the experience of God associated with thunderstorms, a feature to be connected with the third day of creation.

3. It is hardly a proper comparison. The tendency to think of Judaism solely in terms of its ritual law is a strange prejudice. Ignored are the equally important areas such as private law, the law of procedure, family law, and the moral law.

Jewish manner of purifying, and since this water is turned into
wine we have the contrast between a religion that is lower
than the new religion of truth.[4] In other words, to these critics
the water represents the Judaism of Jesus' time which was
characterized by ceremonial observance, and the wine represents a "higher" form of religion which concentrates on spiritual matters. Yet we note that Jesus directs the servants to fill
the pots with water. He does not break or discard these pots,
and thus the imagery used in the tale does not fit too well with
such a broad and sweeping contrast between two religions.
Nor is the contrast that the steward of the banquet makes between the old and the new wine all that strong. In fact, it is
quite benign. He even emphasizes that the drinkers of the second round of wine will hardly notice the difference. Usually,
when interpreters resort to large perspectives, they are admit-
ting, as Dodd does, the difficulties of breaking into the substance of the story.

An approach through the creation story might prove more
illuminating. As in that story up to the third day, so in John
up to this miracle story water plays an important role. If we
assume that the events at Cana somehow mirror the activity of
day three of Gen 1:9–13, much that is suggestive emerges for
a great many details of the Johannine pericope. For example,
the first time that a concern with fertility emerges in the Genesis creation story is on day three: the union of earth and water
to bring forth the fruits of the earth. John's description of how
Jesus uses water in the *stone* pots to produce the juice of the
vine is the equivalent of the union of water and earth on day
three of creation. We might note how the focus of the story is
not on the bride and groom but on the water that is turned
into wine. In some rabbinic circles of John's time, in the cosmological speculation that is inspired by the creation story, the
water of day three of Genesis represents the masculine, gen-
erative source of life and the receiving earth is female (e.g.,
Gen. Rabba 13:13, 14; *y. Taan.* 64b).[5]

---

4. Dodd, *Interpretation*, 297–300.
5. See Hugo Odeberg, *The Fourth Gospel Interpreted in Its Relation to Contempora-*

Philo's understanding of the miraculous nature of what took place on the third day of creation—he compares the dry land to a fertile woman (*De Opic.* 38, 39; *De Plant.* 15)—is directly pertinent to the miracle at Cana. Philo states, "And after a fashion quite contrary to the present order of Nature all the fruit trees were laden with fruit as soon as ever they came into existence" (*De Opic.* 40). The author of 2 Esd 6:43, 44 describes how on day three of creation God's word went forth, "And at once the work was done. For immediately fruit came forth in endless abundance and of varied appeal to the taste." David Winston persuasively argues that in Wis 19:7 the "leafy plain" that emerged when the Israelites crossed the Red Sea at the time of the exodus from Egypt is a continuation in this section of Wisdom 19 of the motif of a refashioning of the days of creation in Genesis 1, in this instance the third day (Gen 1:11–13).[6]

In the close parallel of John's story water has turned into a great abundance of wine—so much wine that its quantity is out of all proportion to the needs of a village wedding at which, moreover, they have already imbibed—without the intermediate processes involving the planting, watering, growth, and harvesting of vines. Philo's comment in *De Opic.* 40 (*Ques Gen* 2.47) contrasts the ordinary way of things: "For now the processes take place in turn, one at one time, one at another, not all of them simultaneously at one season." Nothing in John's narrative suggests how the miracle was brought about: no act of Jesus other than his word is required, as is true again at Cana when he heals the nobleman's son (Jn 4:49–53)—and as was true at the creation of the world when, according to John, Jesus as the Word made all things (Jn 1:3).[7]

---

neous Religious Currents in Palestine and the Hellenistic-Oriental World (Uppsala, 1929), 48–71. He attributes the rabbinic speculation to a time before John.

6. David Winston, *The Wisdom of Solomon*, AB (New York, 1979), 325.

7. In producing the miracle, Jesus gives instructions to the servants at the wedding. For Philo parts of the universe were made to serve God's purpose in the way in which a slave ministers to a master (*Mos.* 1.202).

Water and wine are indeed associated with day three of creation when the waters under the firmament were gathered together into one place, and the dry land—and the fruit trees—appeared. The link between wine and the events of the third day of creation is explicit in the hymn to God the creator in Ps 104:14, 15: "He causeth [on day three of creation] the grass to grow . . . and wine that maketh glad the heart of man." In his discussion of Noah as the first tiller of the soil, when he planted the first vineyard, Philo states that agriculture began with Noah—and on day three of creation (*Ques Gen* 2.66).

In the description of the third day of creation in 2 Esd 6:42—a work that is generally dated around the time of the composition of the Fourth Gospel—the focus is on God's command to assign one-seventh of the space to water and the remaining six parts to dry land. As Joan E. Cook points out, the coming forth of vegetation results from this command but not from a direct command.[8] Moreover, unlike the account in Gen 1:12, 2 Esd 6:44 specifies that the resulting plants had taste, color, and scent. In the incident at Cana of Galilee Jesus' only command is that the waterpots be filled with water. What follows is that, something having occurred indirectly to this water, it now has the taste of wine.

What is also worth pointing out in the Fourth Gospel is how Jesus has the water fetched and poured into the waterpots and how the amount could be measured. According to *Gen. Rabba* 5:1, God used a standard of measurement for the waters that were gathered together into one place at creation (cp. Job 38:5–8; Isa 40:12; 2 Esd 16:57, 58). Equally interesting is the rabbis' understanding of the miracle whereby God poured the water that had covered all the world into one place. To draw out exactly what the miracle was, the rabbis used the following illustration with waterpots. Man empties a full waterpot into an empty one. God emptied a full waterpot into a full one. That

---

8. Joan E. Cook, "Creation in 4 Ezra: The Biblical Theme in Support of Theodicy," in *Creation in the Biblical Traditions*, ed. R. J. Clifford and J. J. Collins, CBQMS 24 (Washington, 1992), 133.

was the nature of the miracle when the waters were gathered together. The rabbis' thinking, presumably, is that after the second day of creation water was everywhere under the firmament. The next day God miraculously moved all of this water into a lesser area without creating a deeper place to accommodate it all. The result was the dry land in one place and the water in another. It is as if a man takes a full pot of water and pours it into another full pot which is miraculously able to accommodate it. In the rabbis' implicit metaphor, the resulting empty pot is the dry land of day three of creation.

I am suggesting that in citing waterpots in his story John uses a metaphor similar to the one used by the rabbis to allude to day three of creation. John's text, which explicitly draws attention to the fullness of the pots: "Fill the waterpots with water. And they [the servants] filled them up to the brim" (Jn 2:7), is comparable to the rabbis' explanation of the miracle of fullness on day three of creation. Full pots of water miraculously become full pots of wine.

The fact that there are six waterpots in John's account may reveal an interesting link to a view found in 2 Esd 6:42: the waters that were gathered together into one place at creation came from six out of the seven parts of the entire area of water that was under the heaven.[9] In other words, six parts of water were poured into one already filled part and in the place of the six appeared land to be cultivated. Since the development occurred immediately ("For thy word went forth, and at once the work was done" [vs. 43]), what had been water instantly became fruitful abundance ("For immediately fruit came forth in endless abundance" [vs. 44]).[10] We should perhaps under-

9. The author of this section of 2 Esdras was a Palestinian Jew, who wrote around the time of the composition of John's Gospel. For another comparison between a cistern and the sea, note Sir 50:3.

10. Milton Horne, William Jewell College, Liberty, Missouri, drew my attention to this possible link between the six waterpots and the passage in 2 Esdras when he was a participant in a seminar for college professors I directed for the National

stand that the pots used by Jesus already have water in them, as a literal reading of the Greek suggests (Jn 2:6), and that more water is then poured into them. If so, the parallel might be with God's activity on day three when he poured water into water.[11]

It is always difficult to know when to cease imputing significance to details in John's narrative, but the location of the miracle at Cana of Galilee can be viewed as a place on dry land between two seas, the sea of Galilee and the Mediterranean. The name Cana, which Birger Olsson thinks is significant and which may derive from *qanah* "to create," might tie into this observation about Cana's location.[12] Cana, this "created place," recalls how at creation dry land appeared. The symbolical significance attributed to places in John's topographical references by second-century exegetes of John's Gospel would suggest that these interpreters, for example, Heracleon,[13] were extending a process already begun in the Gospel, for example, Jn 9:7, which reads, "Go wash in the pool of Siloam, which is translated having been sent." As Thomas Brodie well states, "While the theological dimension of John's cities is strong, their hold on history is often fragile."[14]

Another line of interpretation also leads us to the theme of fertility that is the topic of the third day of creation. John com-

---

Endowment for the Humanities at Cornell University in 1992 on "Law and Religion in the Bible."

11. Commentators, for example, R. E. Brown, *The Gospel According to John I–XII*, AB (New York, 1966), 100, are puzzled by the use of the verb *antlēsate* in reference to drawing water from the pots. The verb is normally used to refer to drawing water from a well (Jn 4:7, 15), that is, the water lodged in the earth. B. F. Westcott, *The Gospel According to St. John* (London, 1908), 84, goes so far as to suggest that the water came from a well and not from the pots. The point is, I think, that the verb is employed because the water and the pots symbolize the water and earth of the created order.

12. Birger Olsson, *Structure and Meaning in the Fourth Gospel* (Lund, 1974), 26.

13. See E. H. Pagels, *The Johannine Gospel in Gnostic Exegesis: Heracleon's Commentary on John* (Nashville, 1973), 52.

14. Thomas Brodie, *The Quest for the Origin of John's Gospel* (Oxford, 1993), 161.

ments that what happened at Cana is the first of the signs Jesus did by way of manifesting his glory, and "his disciples believed on him." The words of the steward to the bridegroom convey the sign: how he, the bridegroom, gave first the good wine, but now he provides the best and not, as is the customary way of bridegrooms, the less good. The significance of the development is that Jesus himself is to be thought of as a bridegroom. He, after all, provided the outstanding wine. We should note that the words of the Baptist in Jn 3:29 well convey the notion of Jesus as a bridegroom: "He that hath the bride is the bridegroom: but the friend [the Baptist] of the bridegroom, which standeth and heareth him, rejoiceth greatly because of the bridegroom's voice: this my joy therefore is fulfilled." When John writes as the climax to the episode that the disciples believed in him, he is suggesting that Jesus, the bridegroom, and his disciples became one, along the lines of a marital union.

The symbolism of the vine permeates the account of the water turned into wine at Cana. In the Old Testament the vine is a well-established symbol of a woman as a wife and mother, for example, a man's wife is a fruitful vine (Ps 128:3).[15] When Jesus says to his mother, "Woman, what have I to do with thee? mine hour is not yet come" (Jn 2:4), we are dealing with what John thinks of as the lower order of creation. She is his mother, a vine, that gave him birth, an act of lower, that is, earthly creation. The use of the designation "Woman," so problematic to interpreters,[16] brings out the fundamental feature that she, a woman, gave birth to a son. This relationship of mother and son is even more explicit in Jn 19:26, "Woman, behold thy son."

---

15. See C. M. Carmichael, *Women, Law, and the Genesis Traditions* (Edinburgh, 1979), 63.

16. In his *Anatomy of the Fourth Gospel* (Philadelphia, 1983), 110, R. Alan Culpepper states, "Whatever the precise connotation of his words to his mother during the wedding at Cana (2:4), there is a certain coldness about them." This attempt, however, to speak about the emotions of Jesus misses the point of the cosmological character of the work. The ideas John works with are primary, their presentation being but a skillful guise.

In rabbinic thought the hour of a man is the hour of his birth.[17] In Jn 16:21 this notion, with the mother's situation as the primary focus, turns up in a context that discusses Jesus' forthcoming resurrection: "A woman when she is in travail hath sorrow, because her hour is come: but as soon as she is delivered of the child, she remembereth no more the anguish, for joy that a man is born into the world." The context is one in which Jesus assures his disciples that their sorrow over his death will be superseded by their joy when they see him again in his risen state. That joyful time will be his hour that was yet to be when he spoke to his mother at the wedding at Cana.[18] Paul's remark in Gal 1:15 is comparable to Jesus' remark to his mother about how his hour has yet to come (Jn 2:4). In discussing the history of his conversion, his becoming newborn, Paul refers to how God "separated him from his mother's womb."[19]

A sequel to the state of unity between Jesus and his disciples is that when his hour (of resurrection) has come he will be glorified "with the glory which I had with thee [his father] before the world was" (Jn 17:1–4). Moreover, he will have glorified his father at that point because he will have completed the work—of re-creation, we might add—that his father had given him to do. John interprets the transformation of the wa-

---

17. Hermann Strack and Paul Billerbeck, *Kommentar zum Neuen Testament aus Talmud und Midrasch* (Munich, 1924), 2:401.

18. Jesus' mother, unnamed, appears in but two scenes (2:1–5, 12; 19:25–27). Culpepper, *Anatomy*, 133, 134, points out how the paucity of description about her has encouraged a variety of symbolic interpretations. He thinks that the overtones of both the scenes in which she appears do indeed point to something very significant. In the second scene she is given over by the dying Jesus to the ideal (the "beloved") disciple. Culpepper cites how Raymond Brown calls these two figures of the mother and the disciple "the two great symbolic figures of the Fourth Gospel." Culpepper continues, "The impact of this scene has been tremendous. Here are the man and 'woman,' the ideal disciple and the mother he is called to receive, standing under the cross of the giver of life. There is the beginning of a new family for the children of God." I would point out that John's underlying theme of procreation is what determines his write-up in both scenes.

19. On this aspect of Paul's conversion, see David Daube, *Appeasement or Resistance; and Other Essays on New Testament Judaism* (Berkeley, 1987), 67, 68.

ter into wine as "This beginning of miracles did Jesus in Cana
of Galilee, and manifested forth his glory" (Jn 2:11). Later in
his Gospel, John gives symbolic expression to the idea of the
unity that exists between Jesus and his disciples when he has
Jesus speak of himself as the true vine and his disciples as its
branches (Jn 15:1–8).

In Jn 2:4, then, when Jesus converses with his mother about
his new "hour" he is implicitly contrasting it with the hour he
experienced with her when she delivered him as her offspring.
He is hinting that the old order of earthly creation is passing
away. His hour, which was actually the hour of his birth, is,
oddly, yet to come: he awaits his new or second birth, the resurrection.

The symbolism of Jesus' mother as the vine that produced
him can be observed from another angle. When she points out
to Jesus that the wedding company has no wine, his response,
"Woman, what have you to do with me, my hour has not yet
come," seems impossibly disconnected. Why should a remark
by a mother to her son about lack of wine prompt the son to
talk about the topic of birth? If the meaning of his remark
about his "hour" has to do with reproduction, as seems certain, we can infer that her reference to wine triggers the underlying symbolism about the vine as a metaphor for human
reproduction.

The mother of Jesus is the vine that produced him. She in
turn anticipates that he will do something with the water, which
he does—he produces wine. Just as she anticipates this sign, so
the sign anticipates something significant to come—he is to be
the vine that produces branches, his disciples. Jesus himself as
a vine thus produces offspring.[20] The sign manifests his glory

---

20. It follows that the disciples are both bride and offspring. Three comments
might be made. One, John does present such contradictions, e.g., Jesus is both
shepherd and gate to the sheepfold. See Dodd, *Fourth Gospel*, 135. Two, a vine as
a metaphor for a human relationship does permit this double significance. The
branches can be thought of as part of the vine in the sense of united with it, as

and, as Dodd claimed, the statement in the prologue is recalled where Christ's glory is that of the only begotten of the Father. The sign at Cana points to the glory he will achieve because those who believe in him, as his disciples do, are begotten of him. We have a remarkable continuity of theme, namely, union and procreation, in all of these manifestly related texts in John.

The incident at Cana closes with a transitional statement about how Jesus goes with his mother and brothers and his disciples to Capernaum. The statement becomes much more significant in meaning in light of John's interplay between the mother who produces sons and Jesus who produces disciples. The imagery of the vine as powerfully reproductive underlies the statement. The apparently simple description about Jesus, his mother, brothers, and disciples constitutes a choice illustration of John's use of a literal statement to bear great meaning, also of a "historical" detail that means much more than meets the eye.[21]

The notion of the vine whose seed is in itself, as described for the third day of creation, may also play a role in John's thinking. In referring to the miracle of day three, Philo states that "the fruit comes out of the plants, as an end out of a beginning, and that out of the fruit again, containing as it does the seed in itself, there comes the plant, a beginning out of an

---

a wife to a husband, but they can also be thought of as the fruit-bearing part of the vine, hence as offspring of the vine. Three, Jesus, in his role as the Word, is the creator of the vine. From this perspective, just as the fruit trees of day three of creation in Genesis appeared simultaneously both as fruitfulness and as fruit-producing, so Jesus' disciples at the same time are both united with him and his offspring.

21. Recall how Philo does not discount the plain meaning of the biblical text but seeks deeper significance: "Some merely follow the outward and obvious . . . I would not censure such persons, for perhaps the truth is with them also. Still, I would exhort them not to halt there, but to press on to allegorical interpretations and to recognise that the letter is to the oracle but as the shadow to the substance, and that the higher values therein revealed are what really and truly exist" (*De Confus.* 190; cp. *De Abr.* 18). I am suggesting that John intends his "outward" statements to be read this way.

end" (*De Opic.* 44). It is tempting to see a similar reflection applied by John to Jesus and his mother. He had a beginning with his mother, but his death will be an end that leads to a beginning, the resurrection. Philo's focus is not dissimilar because of his own particular interest in immortality: "For God willed that Nature should run a course that brings it back to its starting-point, endowing the species with immortality and making them sharers of eternal existence" (*De Opic.* 44). In Jn 3:4 Nicodemus asks Jesus if a man can enter his mother's womb a second time.[22] He misunderstands the higher order of creation. In regard to Jesus and his mother, Jesus will again experience the hour of his birth and simultaneously, along the lines of what miraculously occurred at the first creation, reproduce his own kind, his disciples, who, to borrow Philo's language, will have immortality and share in eternal existence.

John uses a similar line of thinking to Philo's when he describes Jesus' response to some visiting Greeks who sought him out. He focuses their attention on his forthcoming death and rebirth: "Verily, verily, I say unto you, Except a corn of wheat fall into the ground and die, it abideth alone: but if it die, it bringeth forth much fruit" (Jn 12:24).

22. Not in the sense of returning himself but as semen. "The simile is not that of an involution, but of a repetition of the evolution of birth" (Odeberg, *Fourth Gospel*, 48).

Chapter 6

Day Four

(Gen 1:14–19) [14]And God said, Let there be lights in the firmament of the heaven, to divide the day from the night; and
let them be for signs, and for seasons, and for days, and years:
[15]and let them be for lights in the firmament of the heaven,
to give light upon the earth: and it was so. [16]And God made
two great lights; the greater light to rule the day, and the lesser
light to rule the night: he made the stars also. [17]And God set
them in the firmament of the heaven, to give light upon the
earth, [18]and to rule over the day and over the night, and to
divide the light from the darkness: and God saw that it was
good. [19]And the evening and the morning were the fourth day.

(Jn 2:13–3:21) [13]And the Jews' passover was at hand, and Jesus
went up to Jerusalem, [14]And found in the temple those that
sold oxen and sheep and doves, and the changers of money
sitting: [15]And when he had made a scourge of small cords, he
drove them all out of the temple, and the sheep, and the oxen;
and poured out the changers' money, and overthrew the ta-
bles; [16]And said unto them that sold doves, Take these things
hence; make not my Father's house a house of merchandise.
[17]And his disciples remembered that it was written, The zeal of
thine house hath eaten me up. [18]Then answered the Jews and
said unto him, What sign shewest thou unto us, seeing that
thou doest these things? [19]Jesus answered and said unto them,
Destroy this temple, and in three days I will raise it up. [20]Then
said the Jews, Forty and six years was this temple in building,
and wilt thou rear it up in three days? [21]But he spake of the
temple of his body. [22]When therefore he was risen from the

dead, his disciples remembered that he had said this unto
them; and they believed the Scripture, and the word which
Jesus had said. [23]Now when he was in Jerusalem at the passover,
in the feast day, many believed in his name, when they saw the
miracles which he did. [24]But Jesus did not commit himself unto
them, because he knew all men, [25]And needed not that any
should testify of man: for he knew what was in man.

[1]There was a man of the Pharisees, named Nicodemus, a
ruler of the Jews: [2]The same came to Jesus by night, and said
unto him, Rabbi, we know that thou art a teacher come from
God: for no man can do these miracles that thou doest, except
God be with him. [3]Jesus answered and said unto him, Verily,
verily, I say unto thee, Except a man be born again, he cannot
see the kingdom of God. [4]Nicodemus saith unto him, How can
a man be born when he is old? can he enter the second time
into his mother's womb, and be born? [5]Jesus answered, Verily,
verily, I say unto thee, Except a man be born of water and of
the Spirit, he cannot enter into the kingdom of God. [6]That
which is born of the Spirit is spirit. [7]Marvel not that I said unto
thee, Ye must be born again. [8]The wind bloweth where it list-
eth, and thou hearest the sound thereof, but canst not tell
whence it cometh, and whither it goeth: so is every one that is
born of the Spirit. [9]Nicodemus answered and said unto him,
How can these things be? [10]Jesus answered and said unto him,
Art thou a master of Israel, and knowest not these things?
[11]Verily, verily, I say unto thee, We speak that we do know, and
testify that we have seen; and ye receive not our witness. [12]If I
have told you earthly things, and ye believe not, how shall ye
believe, if I tell you of heavenly things? [13]And no man hath
ascended up to heaven but he that came down from heaven,
even the Son of man which is in heaven.

[14]And as Moses lifted up the serpent in the wilderness, even
so must the Son of man be lifted up: [15]That whosoever believeth in him should not perish, but have eternal life. [16]For God
so loved the world, that he gave his only begotten Son, that
whosoever believeth in him should not perish, but have everlasting life. [17]For God sent not his Son into the world to condemn the world; but that the world through him might be
saved.

[18]He that believeth on him is not condemned: but he that

believeth not is condemned already, because he hath not believed in the name of the only begotten Son of God. [19]And
this is the condemnation, that light is come into the world,
and men loved darkness rather than light, because their deeds
were evil. [20]For every one that doeth evil hateth the light, neither cometh to the light, lest his deeds should be reproved.
[21]But he that doeth truth cometh to the light, that his deeds
may be made manifest, that they are wrought in God.

The links between what I claim to be John's fourth day
and day four in Genesis are especially transparent. The initial
description of the fourth day in Genesis determines how John
proceeds to present his account of Jesus' violent action in the
Temple. In Gen 1:14 (cp. Ps 104:19) the first reference to the
meaning of the lights in the firmament is that they are intended to divide the day from the night and to serve as signs,
seasons, days, and years. John's initial focus is on the Passover
of the Jews, an institution that highlights separating the day
from the night and that also combines sign and season. The
lamb is sacrificed in the spring of the year, in the evening, at
the going down of the sun, at the time of the exodus from
Egypt (Deut 16:1–8). The Passover marks the beginning of
months (Exod 12:2, cp *Gen. Rabba* 6:1).[1]

John then proceeds to give explicit focus to the topic of
signs, days, and years, confirmation that he thinks of the Passover as constituting sign and season. He does so in his description of the ensuing discussion between the Jews and Jesus about
the Temple. The Jews react to Jesus' violence in it by requesting
from him a sign to justify his action. Jesus takes up the request
by turning to the topic of the Temple's destruction. He predicts that if the Jews were to destroy the Temple he would raise

1. It is possible that King Hezekiah's cleansing of the Temple served John as
an example for Jesus' action at the beginning of his reign as the "King" of Israel
(Jn 1:49). Hezekiah's action was carried out in the first year of his reign, in the
first month, and was followed by a great Passover celebration (2 Chr 29, 30).
Hezekiah plays an important role as a Messianic type in New Testament times.
See David Daube, *He That Cometh* (London, 1966), 1–5.

it up again in three days.[2] This prediction is unique to John's account of the cleansing of the Temple. There is nothing like it in the Synoptic accounts of the episode (cp. Mk 14:58; Mt 26:61). John's method of recording the history of Jesus as an allegorization of the creation story explains the uniqueness of John's account.

According to Philo, the prediction of future events was made possible by the creation of the heavenly bodies on the fourth day (*De Opic.* 58). In response to Jesus' prediction, the Jews are incredulous. They remind him that the Temple's present structure required forty-six years of effort. Both Jesus and the Jews focus on numbers of days and years. In Philo's comments on day four of creation, he claims that the stars determine the bounds of months and years and "revealed number's place in nature" (*De Plant.* 118). Day four of creation is when the days and years were created, those measures of time that were established by the creation of the greater and lesser lights.

Early Christian interpretation read a symbolic sense into the number forty-six in Jn 2:20. The number was a reference to Adam. The *gematria* of Adam (in Greek initials) gives forty-six. The point of the equation was a cosmological one (*Sibylline Oracles* 3:24–26; 2 En 30:13). The name "Adam" contains the initials of the Greek words for the four cardinal points of the cosmos: *Anatole* (East), *Dysis* (West), *Arktos* (North), and *Mesembria* (South).[3] Such speculation can only arise from an already existing view that the Johannine text has cosmological significance. As just indicated, for Philo, not only were the lights in the firmament to serve as measures of time, but they gave birth to number (*De Opic.* 55, *De Plant.* 118).

Almost all critics agree that John is unhistorical when he

2. The verb is *egeirō*, "to wake up," and, although it can mean "to erect a building," its unexpected choice is determined by the reference to Jesus' resurrection, an awakening from sleep. See David Daube's comments in *Appeasement or Resistance, and Other Essays in New Testament Judaism* (Berkeley, 1987), 12.

3. See Rudolf Schnackenburg, *The Gospel According to St John* (New York, 1968), 1:351; Anthony D. York, "From Biblical Adam to the American Adam: Evolution of a Literary Type," *University of Dayton Review* 21 (1992), 106.

places the incident in the Temple at the beginning of Jesus'
ministry and not at the end, as in the Synoptics. It is important
to ask what motivates John to do so. The explanation may well
lie in his desire to fit the incident into his scheme of days
parallel to those of creation. Most noteworthy is that in John's
time there existed a well-established notion that the Temple
and its contents represented the created universe and its objects. The role of the Temple in cosmological speculation at
this time would explain the peculiar emphasis on the Temple
and its construction in the discussion between Jesus and the
Jews.

The objects of the universe that were created on day four,
the sun, moon, and stars, were thought to belong to God's
temple.[4] God dwells in his created world as in a temple. Josephus states that each of the Temple's objects "is intended to
recall and represent the Universe" (*Ant.* 3.180, *B.J.* 5.212–14).
Philo makes use of temple imagery to describe what was created on the fourth day: "There are images divine and exceed-
ing fair [the heavenly bodies] which he established in heaven
as in the purest temple belonging to corporeal being" (*De Opic.*
55).

From the dialogue between Jesus and the Jews about the
Temple we can infer something of John's particular understanding of it. Jesus and the Jews are both talking about the
Temple at its location in Jerusalem. Jesus, however, directs his
interlocutors' attention to the ideal temple, himself in his res-
urrected state. For John, then, the physical Temple is a sign
pointing to its heavenly form. John's view is probably the one
shared by the author of the Book of Revelation: the Jerusalem
Temple is replaced by God and his Lamb, that is, the risen
Jesus (Rev 21:22, 23). The city has no need of the greater and
lesser light of day four of creation, the sun and the moon—

---

4. See Moshe Weinfeld, "Sabbath, Temple and the Enthronement of the
Lord—The Problem of the Sitz im Leben of Genesis 1:1–2:3," *Festschrift Cazelles*,
AOAT 212 (1981), 506; Peter Hayman, "Some Observations on *Sefer Yesira*: (2)
The Temple at the Centre of the Universe," *JJS* 37 (1986), 176–82.

those markers of days and years—to shine upon it, for the glory of God is its light, and its lamp is the Lamb. Equally interesting in the Book of Revelation is the further echo of the significance of Jesus' cleansing of the Temple in John: nothing impure will ever enter it (Rev 21:27).

When we turn to the next episode in John's Gospel about the visit of Nicodemus to Jesus, the links with day four of creation are equally impressive. We might note first that there is no break in the narrative from what precedes. Although translations (for example, the AV and the RSV) feel the need to state at the opening of the episode that Nicodemus came to Jesus at night, the Greek omits Jesus' name and has simply "came to him" (Jn 3:2).

Commentators see significance in the reference to the visit by night. If the account of day four of creation in Genesis is exerting its influence on John, then we can view the lesser and the greater lights of that day as determining the general framework of the exchange between Nicodemus and Jesus. What John has done in relating his history at this point in his Gospel is both to take his cues from and follow the sequence of what occurred on day four of Gen 1:14–19. Thus he moves from the initial description in Gen 1:14 of the role of the lights in the firmament, namely, they indicate signs, seasons, days, and years—the incident in the Temple—to their role as givers of light upon the earth. This latter role shows up in the respective significance attributed to the ruler of the Jews, Nicodemus, and to Jesus.

That Nicodemus, a ruler of the Jews, comes by night suggests that he represents the lesser light that sees only in the darkness. It is, we are to understand, a light dim by comparison with Jesus, who represents the greater light that rules by day.[5] The Qumran scrolls describe the high priest in the Temple as the "great luminary," that is, the sun (1QSb 4:25–28), and in Sir-

---

5. On Philo's link between the moon and meditation, see *Ques Exod* 1.9. Philo contrasts two kinds of light, one that is perishable and liable to extinction, the other that is imperishable and not liable to extinction (*De Abr.* 157, 158).

ach 50:7 he is the sun (as well as the morning star and the full moon) shining on the Temple.[6] In the *Testament of Naphtali* (5:3–5) Judah is the moon and Levi is the sun. The references are to the Royal and Priestly messiahs respectively. In *Gen. Rabba* 2:3 Jacob is day, Esau night. According to the *Mekhilta* on Exod 18:27, Jethro the father-in-law of Moses is intent on returning to his own land of Midian to enlighten the Midianites about the Torah and to bring them under the wings of the Shechinah. Jethro refers to himself as a lamp, to Moses as the sun, and to Aaron as the moon.[7]

That the symbolism about the lesser and greater lights of the fourth day of creation plays a role in John's narrative emerges all the clearer when we note that its climax is about Jesus as the light that has come into the world (Jn 3:19–21).[8] That light is contrasted with the darkness that men prefer. In preferring darkness they presumably see in their own way because in the created world even the darkness has light, namely, the moon, but it is a lesser light to be disparaged in a manner similar to the way the moon enters the sun's domain and is disparaged (*Gen. Rabba* 6:2). Just before Nicodemus comes to Jesus, John asserts that Jesus did not need to have anyone witness concerning man because Jesus knew what was in man (Jn 2:25). The implication is that his light penetrates man.

The exchange between Nicodemus and Jesus concerns the subject of rebirth by water and the Spirit.[9] Nicodemus cannot

6. See Weinfeld, "Sabbath," 506–7. On the equation in ancient Judaism between astral bodies and human beings, see D. C. Allison, *The New Moses: A Matthean Typology* (Minneapolis, 1993), 152–54.

7. See J. Z. Lauterbach, *Mekhilta de-Rabbi Ishmael* (Philadelphia, 1933), 2: 185–86. On meeting Jesus, Nicodemus speaks in the plural, "We know." The reference could simply be to the Jews he represents. It is interesting, however, that Philo presents the following lineup: the sun is supreme and is contrasted not just with the moon but also with the stars (*De Opic.* 57). Nicodemus's "we" may be linked to the moon and the stars that shine by night.

8. For Philo God created the heavenly bodies to direct attention to the original intellectual light (*De Opic.* 45, 46, 53–57).

9. See Hugo Odeberg's discussion of the terms "water" and "spirit" as signifying elements of "lower" and "higher" creation in cosmological speculation, in

move beyond a literal understanding of birth. For him he thinks of birth in terms of the old order of creation. Philo provides us with the details of that order and, significantly, connects them with day four of creation. He links the birth of human beings with this particular day because birth requires a time span of nine months—and months are associated with day four. Philo further comments on how the stars of day four provide timely signs of coming events and how the appointed times, the seasons of Gen 1:14, he believes, refer to times of achievement such as the birth and growth of creatures (*De Opic.* 59). In his discussion of the flood story, Philo associates the return of life to the earth with the equinox, a season, and therefore he again links birth with day four of creation (*Ques Gen* 2.47). In 2 Esd 6:44, an apocalyptic work roughly contemporary with John, God commands the luminaries of the fourth day of creation to serve man, "who was about to be formed." This phrase, anticipating the birth of man, may well have been prompted by the link between birth and appointed times that Philo is more explicit about.

In Rev 12:1, 2, a sign that appears in heaven is "A woman clothed with the sun, and the moon under her feet, and upon her head a crown of twelve stars. And she being with child cried, travailing in birth, and pained to be delivered."[10] A link with the fourth day of creation surely underlies such a description. The author reveals the same association between birth and the phenomena of the fourth day that we find in Philo and, it would appear, in John too. In Jesus' response to Nicodemus's lower, "earthly" understanding of human birth, Jesus explicitly refers to the heaven above: "And no man hath ascended up to heaven, even the son of man which is in heaven" (Jn 3:13).

The Fourth Gospel Interpreted in Its Relation to Contemporaneous Religious Currents in Palestine and the Hellenistic-Oriental World (Uppsala, 1929), 48–63.

10. According to J. Massyngberde Ford, *Revelation*, AB (New York, 1975), 198, the woman's birth pangs depict the sufferings that precede the coming of the Messiah and the new era.

In the pre-Johannine work, the Book of Jubilees (1:29), we find a comparable interest in the fourth day of creation, new creation, the Temple, and rebirth: "From the day of the creation until the day when the heavens and the earth are renewed and with them all created things both in heaven and on earth, until the day when the sanctuary of the Lord is created in Jerusalem on mount Zion and all the luminaries are renewed as instruments of healing and of peace."

Yet another sign is the subject of the Johannine narrative, but this time it is tied into the subject of rebirth. The sign is Moses' lifting of the serpent in the wilderness. Jesus' ascension into heaven is to be read in this sign. Belief in his transcendent person is what gives new birth, a state of being that will not be subject to death. The sign of the serpent is comparable to the sign of Jesus' violent act in the Temple. Both signs relate to Jesus and both are about destruction, of the Temple and of Jesus respectively. In each instance the sign points forward to new life, again the new temple and the risen Jesus respectively.

How the lifting up of the serpent parallels the lifting up of Jesus into the heavens is not clear. John's cosmological speculation, however, inspired the gnostic interpretation that the serpents of both Num 21:6–9 and Jn 3:14 are stars. The serpent that Moses lifted up is seen in the heaven as light. The serpent's significance is what the opening of John's Gospel refers to: "In the beginning was the Word. . . . All things were made by him." In Hippolyt's recounting of the speculations of the Ophitic sect, the Peratae, he refers to how "The eyes of the blessed see the fair image of the serpent in the great summit [or beginning] of heaven turning about and becoming the source of all movement of all present things. And [the beholder] will know that without him there is nothing framed of heavenly or of earthly things or of things below the earth. . . . In this . . . is the great wonder beheld in the heavens by those who can see."[11]

---

11. Hugo Odeberg's translation, *Fourth Gospel*, 102. Odeberg thinks that most of the interpretation of the passage from Numbers is dependent upon the Fourth Gospel. He also thinks that some of it is pre-Johannine, for example, the inter-

If John uses the scheme of creation in Genesis 1, it is note-worthy that his enumeration of actual days (for example, "And the third day there was a marriage" [Jn 2:1]) ends with the Cana episode that precedes the visit of Nicodemus. John's scheme of relating a succession of days in the life of Jesus is a striking feature that has engendered much comment.[12] Equally striking is that John should stop relating events in this way when the material he goes on to present in his narrative history essentially partakes of the same character. What accounts for this change in his presentation?

The institution of days and time belongs to the fourth day of creation, the day equivalent to John's episodes about the Temple and Nicodemus. John drops at this point in his scheme the enumeration of days characteristic of his description of the life and activity of Jesus so far. That might appear puzzling, a reversal of what we might have expected. In that days and time are associated with the fourth day of creation, we might have expected John to start a scheme similar to his enumeration of the days of Jesus' life in Jn 1:29–2:12, after recounting the episodes about the Temple and Nicodemus.

John, like Philo, however, would not have understood the seven days of creation as days similar to those controlled by the sun and moon. Philo states, "It is quite foolish to think that the world was created in six days or in a space of time at all. Why? Because every period of time is a series of days and nights, and these can only be understood better by the move-ment of the sun as it goes over and under the earth: but the sun is a part of heaven, so that time is confessedly more recent than the world " (*Leg. All.* 1.2, cp. 1.20, *De Opic.* 26, "For time there was not before there was a world"). Creation cannot have

---

pretation of Num 21:8, 9 as "a true and perfect serpent who was also the Me-diator, the Son, the *logos*" (104, 105). Philo has the serpent of Moses a type of the logos (*Leg. All.* 2.79). The important point for my purposes is that so much of John's material indicates cosmological speculation on his part.

12. It is the basis of M.-E. Boismard's thesis that John is laying out an equiva-lent seven days of creation in the life of Jesus, *Du Baptême à Cana* (Paris, 1956). See Chapter 2.

taken place in six natural days, for days are measured by the sun's course and the sun is part of creation. The enumeration of the days of creation in Genesis has nothing to do with quantity. Rather, for Philo, the properties that can be ascribed to individual numbers account for the numbering of the days at the time of creation.[13]

John's understanding of the days referred to in the Genesis account of creation is likely to be similar to Philo's. John's interest is in new creation, to which the idea of eternal time belongs, and therefore contrasts with the old creation. He goes in for chronological sequences of days up to the end of his third "day" of creation and then stops, presumably to bring out this contrast. The point of the contrast is to emphasize the belief that the new creation, though it might recall the old creation, is fundamentally different. The contrast between Nicodemus's understanding of rebirth as requiring an entry into his mother's womb a second time and Jesus' understanding as rebirth through water and the Spirit would constitute something of a parallel.

John's position is well captured in the Book of Revelation. The new Jerusalem no longer has a Temple because it has been replaced by God and the Lamb. The sun and moon, moreover, have become unnecessary (Rev 21:22, 23). It follows that time no longer has a role. In the new order that John and the author of Revelation focus on, a sequence of days is not to be expected because it is a feature of the old order of creation. This view needs to emerge at the point at which there is reflection on the nature of the fourth day of creation.

13. The number 153 in Jn 21:11 is almost certainly an example of numerical symbolism in the Fourth Gospel. See C. K. Barrett, *The Gospel According to St. John* (London, 1955), 581–82.

Chapter 7

Day Five

(Gen 1:20–23) [20]And God said, Let the waters bring forth abundantly the moving creature that hath life, and fowl that may fly above the earth in the open firmament of heaven. [21]And God created great whales, and every living creature that moveth, which the waters brought forth abundantly, after their kind, and every winged fowl after his kind: and God saw that it was good. [22]And God blessed them, saying, Be fruitful, and multiply, and fill the waters in the seas; and let fowl multiply in the earth. [23]And the evening and the morning were the fifth day.

(Jn 3:22–36) [22]After these things came Jesus and his disciples into the land of Judea; and there he tarried with them, and baptized.

[23]And John also was baptizing in Aenon near to Salim, because there was much water there: and they came, and were baptized. [24]For John was not yet cast into prison.

[25]Then there arose a question between some of John's disciples and a Jew about purifying. [26]And they came unto John, and said unto him, Rabbi, he that was with thee beyond Jordan, to whom thou barest witness, behold, the same baptizeth, and all men come to him. [27]John answered and said, A man can receive nothing, except it be given him from heaven. [28]Yourselves bear me witness, that I said, I am not the Christ, but that I am sent before him. [29]He that hath the bride is the bridegroom: but the friend of the bridegroom, which standeth and heareth him, rejoiceth greatly because of the bridegroom's voice: this my joy therefore is fulfilled. [30]He must increase, but I must decrease. [31]He that cometh from above is above all: he that is of the earth is earthly, and

speaketh of the earth: he that cometh from heaven is above all. ³²And what he hath seen and heard that he testifieth; and no man receiveth his testimony. ³³He that hath received his testimony hath set his seal that God is true. ³⁴For he whom God hath sent speaketh the words of God: for God giveth not the Spirit by measure unto him. ³⁵The Father loveth the Son, and hath given all things into his hand. ³⁶He that believeth on the son hath everlasting life: and he that believeth not the Son shall not see life; but the wrath of God abideth on him.

Immediately noteworthy is that in the Genesis account of creation, in its description of the fifth day of creation, the contrast between the waters of the earth and the open firmament of the heaven is strikingly present in the contrast in Jn 3:22–36 between the waters for baptism and the heavenly realm from whence comes enlightenment. John presents the Baptist's activity and his pronouncements as an allegorization of day five of the Genesis creation story.

The water creatures that are brought forth on the fifth day of creation in Genesis have their allegorical counterpart in those who become disciples through baptism by water.[1] The notion is the one expressed in the Synoptics: those who win over others to their master's cause are fishers of men (Mk 1:17; Mt 4:19). In ancient Christian sarcophagi a fisherman became a symbol of baptism.[2]

The identification of the creatures in the waters with human disciples is not so bizarre—and certainly not in an allegorical work—when we recall that Jesus is spoken of as a lamb. We might also note the equation of water to humankind in Rev 17:15: "The waters which thou sawest, where the whore sitteth, are peoples, and multitudes, and nations, and tongues."[3]

1. The Greek version understands Gen 1:20 as a command directed to the waters to spawn fish (*exagagetō*).
2. W. D. Davies and D. C. Allison, *The Gospel According to Saint Matthew*, ICC (Edinburgh, 1988), 1:399.
3. For water as seed, note Num 24:7. Also 2 Bar 57:1: "And after these you saw bright waters: these represent the fount of Abraham and his family, and the coming of his son and of his grandson, and of those like him." When the Sa-

We must always remember that John, like Philo, uses the structural features of the created universe for symbolic purposes. Either Jesus himself baptizes (despite the contrary statement in Jn 4:2), and/or his disciples, and so too does the Baptist. Those baptized by Jesus increase while there is a decrease in those who undergo the water ritual at the hands of the Baptist. Every aspect of John's narrative, with its contrast between what is above and what is of the earth, is illumined once we relate it back to the creation story, in this instance to the contrast between the fowl of the air and the creatures of the water that come forth on the fifth day.

Baptism constitutes a new birth, a topic that we might well expect to recur because of its previous treatment in regard to Nicodemus. Those who produce new beings through baptism are reproducing their own kind. They are being fruitful and multiplying. Baptism is the ceremony by which a convert, becoming Jewish, gives up all his previous ties and is regarded as newly born: "Anyone who brings a gentile near is as though he had created him" (*Gen. Rabba* 12:6). According to *Babylonian Yebamoth* 22a, a convert is "a child just born." Paul speaks of Onesimus as "My child whom I have begot" (Phil 1:10).[4]

One implication of baptism as a new birth is that a person so born becomes the offspring of a parent different from his biological parent. Paul is explicit about such a development in the life of a person (Onesimus). In *Num. Rabba* 8:3 God expresses appreciation of the proselyte who leaves his family and his father's house and, after baptism, enters the family of Israel. Hillel, a strong advocate of proselytization, is quoted as saying, "Be of the disciples of Aaron, loving peace and pursuing peace, loving mankind [literally, the creatures] and bringing them

---

maritans come to believe in Jesus as the Messiah they are compared to plants ready to harvest (Jn 4:35–38).

4. See David Daube, *Appeasement or Resistance, and Other Essays on New Testament Judaism* (Berkeley, 1987), 62.

nigh to the Law" (*Pirqe Aboth* 1:12).⁵ This counsel, probably addressed to his own disciples, exhorts them to make disciples of the gentiles, who are referred to as "the creatures."⁶ The notion of natural creatures who become new creatures through the waters of baptism can be inferred.⁷ According to Mt 28:19 (cp. Mk 16:15, 16), Jesus after his resurrection commands his disciples, "Make disciples of all nations, baptizing them." The profound notion of rebirth in the original ceremony of proselyte baptism was carried over into movements such as the appeal by the Baptist to those already Jewish to repent and prepare for the new age. His specific focus on his fellow Jews is the reason why he was given the name "the Baptist," or "the Baptizer."⁸

Commentators point out that the reference to Jesus' baptismal activity in John is surprising when contrasted with the position in the Synoptics, where the reference to the need of the disciples to baptize converts after the death of their master is in fact the only one.⁹ In Mk 16:15 the language is "Go into all the world and preach the gospel to the whole creation [*ktisei*]," this command being followed by the reference to the disciples' baptismal activity. Despite the paucity of references in the Synoptics to Jesus' concern with baptism, it is nonetheless interesting that this passage in Mark links baptism and creation.

If John relates Jesus to the scheme of creation in Genesis we can understand better not just John's reference to Jesus' bap-

5. "To bring near" is a technical term in Tannaitic language about conversion. See David Daube, *The New Testament and Rabbinic Judaism* (London, 1956), 281.

6. On the connection between the theme of peace and attracting outsiders, see David Daube, "Pauline Contributions to a Pluralistic Culture: Re-creation and Beyond," in *Jesus and Man's Hope*, ed. D. G. Miller and D. Y. Hadidian (Pittsburgh, 1971), 2:223–45.

7. A comparable transformation from one creaturely condition to another is implied in *B.M.* 2:11, in the precedence given to a teacher over a father: "His father did but bring him into this world, but his teacher that taught him wisdom brings him into the world to come."

8. See Daube, *The New Testament and Rabbinic Judaism*, 119.

9. See Rudolf Schnackenburg, *The Gospel According to St John* (New York, 1968), 1:411.

tismal activity (in Jn 3:22) but also the contradictory statement
in Jn 4:2: "Though Jesus himself baptized not, but his disciples." This statement about how only the disciples baptized,
not Jesus, has to be understood, we shall see, in light of John's
equivalent of the sixth day of creation in Gen 1:24–31.

The theme of reproduction turns up in many sections of the
Genesis creation account, for example, the sea and air creatures of day five are to be fruitful and multiply; likewise, the
male and female of day six. Philo states, in regard to many
facets of the different days of creation: "To each of the days
He assigned some of the portions of the whole" (*De Opic.* 15).
John reveals a similar allocation of features to different days in
his presentation. The theme of reproduction, for example, re-
curs in John also. The theme came into the pericope about
the marriage at Cana. At the plain level Jesus is the son of Mary;
at the symbolic level both she and Jesus are vines. The theme
also showed up in the episode about Nicodemus. Reproduction
again comes into reckoning in the description of the Baptist's
and Jesus' baptismal activity: there is increase of converts for
Jesus, decrease for the Baptist.

Reproduction is also the main point of the Baptist's description of himself as the friend of the bridegroom who has occasion to rejoice. Because this description has not been
interpreted this way, it needs to be looked at more closely. The
context for the Baptist's remark concerns baptism and hence
new birth. One can expect from a bridegroom and a bride the
birth of a child. (In the preceding discourse about new birth
between Jesus and Nicodemus there is reference to entering a
mother's womb and being born again.) The Baptist speaks of
his joy in hearing the bridegroom's voice; in fact, he claims
that his joy is now fulfilled and that Jesus must increase while
he must decrease. This reference to increasing suggests pro-
spective offspring for the newlyweds. Much evidence supports
the contention that the Baptist's reference to joy has in mind
not just the pleasure associated with a marriage but the birth
of new life that might follow.

There are numerous examples throughout biblical literature

of the association between joy and childbirth. A Deuteronomic
law grants exemption from military service for one year to a
newly married man so that he can give joy to his wife (Deut
24:5). The meaning is not solely the joy of sex but the birth
of a child that might follow.[10] Jeremiah refers to the occasion
of his birth: a messenger brought news to his father that made
him exceedingly joyful (Jer 20:15). The same expression that
the Baptist uses, "to rejoice greatly," occurs in Isa 66:10. The
unmistakable allusion is to the bearing of children, in this instance, Jerusalem's children.

"To rejoice greatly" is used elsewhere in the Fourth Gospel.
For example, in Jn 15:11 the reference is to Jesus' fruitfulness,
analogous to the Baptist's reference. Jesus is the vine, his disciples the branches, and his father as the vinedresser attends
to their fruit-yielding capacity. To describe the future joy of the
disciples when they learn of Jesus' birthlike resurrection after
he dies, John uses the analogy of what occurs at the actual birth
of a child: "A woman when she is in travail hath sorrow, because her hour is come: but as soon as she is delivered of the
child, she remembereth no more the anguish, for joy that a
man is born into the world" (Jn 16:21). We might recall, in
relation to this statement, how on the occasion of a wedding,
an event synonymous with joy, Jesus alluded to the hour of his
birth in speaking to his mother (Jn 2:4). One other reference,
in this instance to Jesus' joy for his disciples, is worth noting.
C. K. Barrett claims that his statement, "That they [the disci-
ples] might have my joy fulfilled in themselves" (Jn 17:13), is
about the disciples as the offspring of Jesus and their future
fruitfulness as apostles in the world.[11]

The imagery of vines, associated with the third day of creation, plays a role in John's description of the relationship between Jesus and his mother and Jesus and his disciples.

10. See C. M. Carmichael, *The Laws of Deuteronomy* (Ithaca, 1974), 208, 209;
also *The Return of the Divorcee* (Inaugural Jewish Law Fellowship Lecture, Oxford
Centre for Postgraduate Hebrew Studies, Oxford, 1992), 27, 28.

11. See C. K. Barrett, *The Gospel According to St. John* (London, 1955), 421–22.

Likewise, the imagery of the water creatures of the fifth day of creation underlies John's depiction of the Baptist's understanding of his use of water.

A different facet of the fifth day of creation shows up in Jn 3:25. This text baldly refers to a discussion about purification between the disciples of the Baptist and a Jew.[12] C. K. Barrett thinks that the reference to purification is not the baptism performed by John the Baptist, nor that performed by Jesus, but to Jewish purification in general.[13] The text of Jn 3:25 gives no indication as to the substance of the discussion. In light of the Baptist's response to his disciples, however, in which he contrasts earthly matters with heavenly, we can reasonably assume that John intends the discussion about purification to constitute an example of an earthly concern about the distinction between clean and unclean creatures.

The discussion about purification between these disciples and the Jew would be most appropriate in the context of a comprehension of the fifth day of creation. The reason is that the clean and unclean water creatures and the birds of the sacrificial and dietary rules in Lev 11:9–19 and Deut 14:9–20 have a fundamental link to day five of creation. On that day they came into existence.[14] Not surprisingly, Philo discusses the rules of Leviticus 11 about unclean and clean creatures in terms of the earthly and the heavenly (*De Mig.* 64, 65; *De Leg.* 4.110–12). The Baptist's response to his disciples likewise focuses on this distinction.[15]

The fifth day of creation produced the fowls of the air as

---

12. The singular "Jew" is likely to be the original reading.

13. Barrett, *St. John*, 221.

14. For a recent attempt to analyze these rules in relation to Genesis 1—"The dietary laws systematically pick up the order of creation in Genesis"—see Mary Douglas, "The Forbidden Animals in Leviticus," *JSOT* 59 (1993), 16–18. (She has the earth created on day one instead of day three which, in turn, she erroneously attributes to the texts in Gen 1:11–13 instead of to 1:9–13.)

15. According to rabbinic sources, on the fifth day of creation God consigned the lower waters, from which the water creatures were brought forth, to a place of uncleanness: see M. M. Kasher, *Encyclopedia of Biblical Interpretation* (New York, 1953), 1: no. 147.

well as the water creatures beneath. In John, the concluding discourse, supposedly issuing from the Baptist, is also about a distinction between the upper and the lower. The Baptist contrasts what comes from heaven with what is of the earth. The type from above communicates heavenly knowledge because the Spirit has imparted it to him. The one preceding time that the Baptist makes mention of the Spirit is at the baptism of Jesus. On that occasion he likens its descent to a bird of the air, the dove. The allusion is to the movement of the Spirit that hovered over the water on day one of creation. Philo's view about the interrelatedness of each day of creation ("To each of the days He assigned some of the portions of the whole" [*De Opic.* 15]) is again pertinent to John's procedure.

The link between the dove and the Spirit, and hence between the birds of the air and heavenly knowledge, is also a feature of the symbolism that Philo applies to the physical universe. He has the birds represent incorporeal and divine forms of knowledge: "It is a special property of divine wisdom that it ever soars aloft like a bird" (*Her.* 130–32 and 215). Air is the abode of incorporeal beings (*Som.* 1.135). In one of Philo's discussions he contrasts the way animals can be symbolically divided into opposites, to represent truth and falsity, for example, with the inability so to divide birds: "The birds He [God] left undivided, for incorporeal and divine forms of knowledge cannot be divided into conflicting opposites" (*Her.* 132). A similar contrast may underlie John's narrative. There is the issue of purification with its presumed fundamental focus on the division into what is clean and what is unclean. This aspect of things stands in contrast to the significance of the Spirit: "He [God] gives [the Spirit] not by measure" (Jn 3:34). The Church Father Origen interpreted the statement to mean that the Spirit is given not in part but in unlimited, undivided fullness (*Commentarii in Jn* 3:34).

The discourse in Jn 3:31–36 contrasting earthly and heavenly matters concludes with a judgment on the person who does not believe the Son's heavenly testimony. Upon that unbeliever "the wrath of God abideth" (vs. 36). The Book of Revelation

presents very similar sentiments and, interestingly for our purposes, these are all couched in cosmological language. In its
vision of cosmological events we find, to choose but one example, the angel that flies in midheaven and proclaims an eternal gospel to those who sit on the earth: "Fear God and give
glory to him; for the hour of his judgment is come: and worship
him that made heaven, and earth, and the sea and the foun-
tains of water" (Rev 14:7). Another angel predicts that those
who worship the beast that had arisen out of the sea (Rev
13:1) will drink the wine of God's wrath (Rev 14:9, 10). The
text of Revelation goes on to contrast the monster from the
sea with another monster that rises out of the land (Rev 13:
11). These two monsters represent the two mythical creatures
Leviathan and Behemoth that, according to Jewish tradition
(e.g., 2 Esd 6:49), God created on the fifth day of creation.[16]
The author of the Book of Revelation, like Philo, and, I am
arguing, John too, allegorizes the water creatures and the flying
creatures of the air to represent human and divine attributes.

To summarize, in Gen 1:20–23, the fifth day of creation,
there are the creatures that came out of the water and those
that fly in the open firmament of the heaven. There is also the
blessing on them to be fruitful and multiply. John's corresponding interests are the Baptist's baptizing at Aenon "because there was much water there" (Jn 3:23); the discussion
about purification; the focus on the contrast between the upper realm and the lower; and the increase in numbers (of converts).

16. See G. B. Caird, *The Revelation of St. John the Divine*, BNTC (London, 1966),
161.

Chapter 8

Day Six

(Gen 1:24–31) ²⁴ And God said, Let the earth bring forth the living creature after his kind, cattle, and creeping thing, and beast of the earth after his kind: and it was so. ²⁵And God made the beast of the earth after his kind, and cattle after their kind, and every thing that creepeth upon the earth after his kind: and God saw that it was good. ²⁶And God said, Let us make man in our image, after our likeness: and let them have dominion over the fish of the sea, and over the fowl of the air, and over the cattle, and over all the earth, and over every creeping thing that creepeth upon the earth. ²⁷So God created man in his own image, in the image of God created he him: male and female created he them. ²⁸And God blessed them, and God said unto them, Be fruitful, and multiply, and replenish the earth, and subdue it: and have dominion over the fish of the sea, and over the fowl of the air, and over every living thing that moveth upon the earth. ²⁹And God said, Behold, I have given you every herb bearing seed, which is upon the face of all the earth, and every tree, in the which is the fruit of a tree yielding seed: to you it shall be for meat. ³⁰And to every beast of the earth, and to every fowl of the air, and to every thing that creepeth upon the earth, wherein there is life, I have given every green herb for meat: and it was so. ³¹And God saw every thing that he had made, and, behold, it was very good. And the evening and the morning were the sixth day.

(Jn 4:1–54) ¹ When therefore the Lord knew how the Pharisees had heard that Jesus made and baptized more disciples than John, ²(Though Jesus himself baptized not, but his disciples,) ³He left Judea, and departed again into Galilee. ⁴And he must needs go through Samaria. ⁵Then cometh he to a city of Samaria, which is called Sychar, near to the parcel of ground that Jacob gave to his son Joseph. ⁶Now Jacob's well was there. Jesus therefore, being wearied with his journey, sat thus by the well [on the ground]: and it was about the sixth hour. ⁷There cometh a woman of Samaria to draw water: Jesus saith unto her, Give me to drink. ⁸(For his disciples had gone away unto the city to buy meat.) ⁹Then saith the woman of Samaria unto him, How is it that thou, being a Jew, askest drink of me, which am a woman of Samaria? for the Jews have no dealings with the Samaritans. ¹⁰Jesus answered and said unto her, If thou knewest the gift of God, and who it is that saith to thee, Give me to drink; thou wouldest have asked of him, and he would have given thee living water. ¹¹The woman saith unto him, Sir, thou hast nothing to draw with, and the well is deep: from whence then hast thou that living water? ¹²Art thou greater than our father Jacob, which gave us the well, and drank thereof himself, and his children, and his cattle? ¹³Jesus answered and said unto her, Whosoever drinketh of this water shall thirst again: ¹⁴But whosoever drinketh the water that I shall give him shall never thirst; but the water that I shall give him shall be in him a well of water springing up into everlasting life. ¹⁵The woman saith unto him, Sir, give me this water, that I thirst not, neither come hither to draw. ¹⁶Jesus saith unto her, Go, call thy husband, and come thither. ¹⁷The woman answered and said, I have no husband. Jesus said unto her, Thou hast well said, I have no husband: ¹⁸For thou hast had five husbands; and he whom thou now hast is not thy husband: in that saidst thou truly. ¹⁹The woman saith unto him, Sir, I perceive that thou art a prophet. ²⁰Our fathers worshipped in this mountain; and ye say, that in Jerusalem is the place where men ought to worship. ²¹Jesus saith unto her, Woman, believe me, the hour cometh, when ye shall neither in this mountain, nor yet at Jerusalem worship the Father. ²²Ye worship ye know not what: we know what we worship; for salvation is of the Jews. ²³But the hour cometh, and now is, when the true worshippers shall worship the Father in spirit and in truth: for the Father seeketh such to worship him. ²⁴God is a Spirit: and they that worship him must worship him in spirit and in truth. ²⁵The woman saith unto him, I know that Messias cometh, which is called Christ: when he is come, he will tell us all things. [26]Jesus saith unto her, I that speak unto thee am he.

[27]And upon this came his disciples, and marvelled that he talked with the woman: yet no man said, What seekest thou? or, Why talkest thou with her? [28]The woman then left her waterpot, and went her way into the city, and saith to the men, [29]Come, see a man, which told me all things that ever I did: is not this the Christ? [30]Then they went out of the city, and came unto him.

[31]In the mean while his disciples prayed him, saying, Master, eat. [32]But he said unto them, I have meat to eat that ye know not of. [33]Therefore said the disciples one to another, Hath any man brought him aught to eat? [34]Jesus saith unto them, My meat is to do the will of him that sent me, and to finish his work. [35]Say not ye, there are yet four months, and then cometh harvest? behold, I say unto you, Lift up your eyes, and look on the fields; for they are white already to harvest. [36]And he that reapeth receiveth wages, and gathereth fruit unto life eternal: that both he that soweth and he that reapeth may rejoice together. [37]And herein is that saying true, One soweth, and another reapeth. [38]I sent ye to reap that whereon ye bestowed no labour: other men laboured, and ye are entered into their labours.

[39]And many of the Samaritans of that city believed on him for the saying of the woman, which testified, He told me all that ever I did. [40]So when the Samaritans were come unto him, they besought him that he would tarry with them: and he abode there two days. [41]And many more believed because of his own word; [42]And said unto the woman, now we believe, not because of thy saying: for we have heard him ourselves, and know that this is indeed the Christ, the Saviour of the world.

[43]Now after two days he departed thence, and went into Galilee. [44]For Jesus himself testified, that a prophet hath no honour in his own country. [45]Then when he was come into Galilee, the Galileans received him, having seen all the things that he did at Jerusalem at the feast: for they also went unto the feast. [46]So Jesus came again into Cana of Galilee, where he made the water wine. And there was a certain nobleman, whose son was sick at Capernaum. [47]When he heard that Jesus had come out of Judea into Galilee, he went unto him, and

besought him that he would come down, and heal his son: for he was at the point of death. [48]Then said Jesus unto him, Except ye see signs and wonders, ye will not believe. [49]The nobleman saith unto him, Sir, come down ere my child die. [50]Jesus saith unto him, Go thy way, thy son liveth. And the man believed the word that Jesus had spoken unto him, and he went his way. [51]And as he was now going down, his servants met him, and told him, saying, Thy son liveth. [52]Then inquired he of them the hour when he began to amend. And they said unto him, Yesterday at the seventh hour the fever left him. [53]So the father knew that it was at the same hour, in the which Jesus said unto him, Thy son liveth: and himself believed, and his whole house. [54]This is again the second miracle that Jesus did, when he was come out of Judea into Galilee.

Four correspondences between day six of John's presentation and day six of Gen 1:24–31 are noteworthy. One, in Genesis on the sixth day the earth brings forth the land animals, after their kind, the day after the production of the water creatures. In John's sixth day the disciples of Jesus produce, after their kind, other disciples. Unlike the Baptist, in his baptismal activity that corresponds to the fifth day of Genesis, there is no mention of the use of water when the disciples of Jesus baptize. All that we are told is that Jesus' disciples baptize in the land of Judea (Jn 3:22), information that John comments on in Jn 4:1, 2. Commentators are at pains to stress that their baptismal activity is of a different order from the Baptist's.[1] By portraying the disciples as creating converts by baptism in the land of Judea but not mentioning water, John allegorizes the sixth day of creation when living creatures came forth from the land without the involvement of water.

The reference to Jacob's animals at the well (Jn 4:12) is a plain tie-in to this sixth day when the land animals were created. What we find is the typical Johannine back and forth

1. E.g., Rudolf Schnackenburg, *The Gospel According to St John* (New York, 1968), 1:410–12.

between allegorical and literal meaning. Both the creatures of the sea of day five and the land animals of day six come to represent human beings. The allegorization of the creatures of sea and land is a characteristic of the Book of Revelation (e.g., Rev 5:6; 13).

John's narrative takes on a different complexion if we assume his focus is on the activity associated with the earth or land—referred to no less than eleven times—on day six of creation in Gen 1:24–31. His narrative shows a comparable emphasis on the earth or land. Jesus takes a journey that traverses the land from Judea to Galilee. The journey is through a specific part of the earth, Samaria. It includes the ground given to Joseph by Jacob and on which is the well at which Jacob's animals watered. The more difficult reading—and hence the one that is probably original—of Jn 4:6, *epi tē gē,* "[he sat] on the ground," as against the reading *epi tē pēgē,* "by the well," becomes most interesting in light of the focus on the earth of day six. The creator of the world, Jesus, is involved again with that part of it, the earth, on which the land animals came forth on day six of the Genesis account of creation.

John presents the various baptisms on the part of the Baptist, the disciples of Jesus, and Jesus himself in a markedly different way from the way in which the Synoptic Gospels present baptismal activity by these parties. In the Synoptics there is no mention of any such activity by Jesus or his disciples other than Jesus' injunction to his disciples after his resurrection to baptize (Mt 28:19, cp. Mk 16:16). If we bear in mind that for John (as for other Jews of the time) baptism is a form of creation and reproduction, the clue to his account of the various baptisms is his allegorical treatment of the different forms of creative activity on days five and six of creation in Genesis. Philo illumines John's thinking.

For Philo there are distinctions to be made among the living creatures of days five and six according to their level of worth: "For when the Creator determined to form living creatures, those first in order were inferior, if we may so speak, namely

fishes, while those that came last in order were best, namely
men; and coming between the two extremes, better than those
that preceded them, but inferior to the others, were the rest,
namely land creatures and birds of the air" (*De Opic.* 68).[2]
John's ranking of the different baptisms and the consequences
that he describes for them may be along lines similar to Philo's
ranking of the creatures on days five and six of creation. For
the evangelist the Baptist's use of water to give birth to his
disciples corresponds to the level of creatures created on day
five, namely, the water creatures. The disciples of Jesus in turn
give birth to disciples, and their baptismal activity in the land
of Judea corresponds to that of the land creatures that were
created on day six. The fact that the Baptist directs his disciples
to Jesus (Jn 1:40–46), which would mean that they become
disciples of Jesus, indicates that they attain a higher level of
worth because of their new allegiance.[3]

Philo emphasizes that all creatures share something in common. For example, he points out that insofar as man dwells
and moves on the ground, he is a land animal; insofar as he
swims and sails, he is a water creature; insofar as his "body
ascends and is raised aloft from the earth," he is an "air-
walker"; insofar as sight is the most dominant of his senses and
can cause him to be drawn to the heavenly bodies, he is heavenly (*De Opic.* 147). The perception of such shared features
among the different creatures makes it easier for an allegorist
such as Philo, and John too presumably, to move back and
forth between the human and nonhuman worlds. In fables,
plants and animals, while retaining their essential characteris-

2. On this reading of Genesis, Philo gives the birds a lesser role than in other
readings of his, for example, when he discusses how birds represent incorporeal
and divine forms of knowledge (*Her.* 132). We should remember that Philo is a
consummate exponent of the art of finding several meanings in the same text.

3. The Pharisees are upset by Jesus' activity (Jn 4:1–3). According to Gen 1:
28, all of the lower creatures of the sea, air, and land were to be subjected to
human dominion. Conceivably, in John since these new disciples give their allegiance to Jesus, we are to understand that Jesus threatens the dominion of the
Pharisees.

tics, are given human traits so as to convey messages about the world of human affairs. The reason why fables communicate such messages so well is precisely because what goes on in the world of plants and animals comes near enough to what goes on in the human world to invite comparison.

Two, in Genesis man is made in God's image, male and female "created he them." In John the male-female aspect of Jesus' meeting with the Samaritan woman is highlighted: for example, her marital history is gone into, and Jesus' presence with her as a male in the absence of any other person occasions surprise in the disciples.

The Baptist produces new beings by water baptism at a level that corresponds to the activity of day five of creation. The disciples of Jesus produce new beings at a level that corresponds to the land creatures of day six. Jesus in turn produces at the highest level. He re-creates the Samaritan woman by making her a well of living water. Her re-creation harks back to the creation of the male-female relationship of the sixth day of creation.

The way John presents this aspect is extraordinarily subtle. She meets Jesus at Jacob's well at high noon, precisely the odd time—as commentators point out, it is the hottest part of the day and consequently avoided—when the patriarch Jacob met his future wife Rachel (Gen 29:7).[4] Jesus is alone with her, and one indication that we are meant to focus on the sexual nature of the encounter is the later reflection of the disciples that they "marvelled that he talked with the woman" (Jn 4:27).

The conversation about the water at the well between Jesus and the woman turns on the sexual symbolism attaching to water. Water is proverbially associated with female sexuality. The counsel given to a married man includes: "Drink waters out of thine own cistern, and running waters out of thine own well" (Prov 5:15); "Let thy fountain be blessed: and rejoice with the wife of thy youth" (Prov 5:18, cp. Prov 9:17, "Stolen

4. John Bligh, "Jesus in Samaria," *HJ* 3 (1962), 336, drew attention to this parallel with Jacob's marriage.

waters are sweet"). The counsel is to the end that a husband may steer clear of "strange women." When Jesus asks the female stranger at the well, "Give me to drink," he is using the language of sexual love.[5] When he invites her to partake of "living water," so that she will become "a well of living water," at one level he is speaking of her sexuality along the lines of the bride in the Song of Songs who is similarly described (Cant 4:12). Hugo Odeberg demonstrates just how rich "water" as a procreative symbol is in the rabbinic and Hellenistic literature that is pertinent to the mystical concepts that show up in the Fourth Gospel. For example, the upper waters in 1 En 54:8, *Gen. Rabba* 13:13, 14, are the celestial, male water, while the waters beneath the earth, well water, for example, are the feminine.[6]

Decisive confirmation that sexual symbolism associated with water is playing a major role in the narrative about the Samaritan woman comes from pondering how the subject of the woman's marital history—bewilderingly, it would appear—comes into the conversation. After she requests to become a well of living water, Jesus asks her to call her husband. When she responds by saying that she has no husband he informs her that she has had five. We can only grasp the sense of the narrative by following through on the sexual symbolism of the conversation about water. Five men, so to speak, had previously asked her, "Give me to drink," and she had duly distributed her "water" to each in turn.

In characteristic fashion the evangelist switches from the down-to-earth meaning to an elevated one. When, oddly, Jesus says to her, "And now he whom thou hast is not thine husband" (Jn 4:18), he probably means himself. He is removing

5. As I pointed out in "Marriage and the Samaritan Woman," *NTS* 26 (1980), 336 n. 16, the term "water" in Jesus' request to the Samaritan woman, "Give me to drink," is understood and is consequently one clue that a figurative sense is intended.

6. Hugo Odeberg, *The Fourth Gospel Interpreted in Its Relation to Contemporaneous Religious Currents in Palestine and the Hellenistic-Oriental World* (Uppsala, 1929), 51–68.

himself from an ordinary sexual association with her so that she comprehends who he really is. Her response to his talk about husbands is "Sir, I perceive that thou art a prophet" (Jn 4:19). He is more than that, as she comes to appreciate. Not only is he greater than the patriarch Jacob who had met his bride at the place Jesus and she stand (Jn 4:12). As emerges in a later contretemps with the Jews when they claim that he is a Samaritan (Jn 8:48–58), he is greater also than Abraham: "Before Abraham was, I am" (Jn 8:58). He is in fact above the level of ordinary male-female sexuality because as the Word at creation he is the one who originally created the first man, "male and female created he them."[7]

The switch from Jesus' sexual relationship to the woman to his role as her creator has a parallel in a rabbinic interpretation of Prov 5:15, the plain meaning of which is about sexual relations between a man and his wife. The text, as Hugo Odeberg points out, came to be interpreted as "Drink waters out of thine own cistern [*boreka*], that is, drink of the waters of thy Creator [*bore'eka*]."[8] Philo also provides a parallel to the thought that underlies the woman's transformation from a deformed order of living to a higher spiritual one when he comments about Moses' second birth. Moses' first birth came from a "body and had corruptible parents," whereas his second birth was a divine one, which had no mother but only a father, God (*Ques Exod* 2.46).[9]

Three, in Genesis the blessing upon the male and the female on the sixth day of creation is to result in their being fruitful and multiplying. In John, after the personal encounter between Jesus and the Samaritan woman, there is no more mention of any man in the woman's life. Nonetheless, she produces off-

7. As I noted for the relationship between Jesus and his disciples in the context of the wedding at Cana, Jesus is again both bridegroom and the one who gives birth to the bride. His role as the preexistent Word and as a historical being accounts for this rather bewildering manner of thinking.

8. Odeberg, *Fourth Gospel*, 159.

9. This reborn Moses represents pure mind (*ho katharōtatos nous*). *Au fond*, what the Samaritan woman's mind believes is what makes her a new being.

spring—in the sense of new believers in Jesus as the Messiah.[10]
In her new state of re-creation, she goes to her own people and
wins them over: a multiplication of believers.

Jesus' involvement with a woman might have been expected
because of the Baptist's earlier, anticipatory comment about
how he, the Baptist, is but the friend of the bridegroom (Jn
3:29). He means Jesus as bridegroom (cp. Mk 2:19). When the
Baptist goes on to state how Jesus must increase but he decrease, namely, in the numbers of disciples each will have, the
underlying idea is the number of offspring that comes from a
marital union. The multiplication of believers that results from
Jesus' involvement with the Samaritan woman is exactly what
the Baptist anticipated and harks back to the blessing of the
sixth day of creation that the male and the female should be
fruitful and multiply.

In a noticeably abrupt change of direction John switches
from a description of the earthly male-female aspect of Jesus'
relationship to the Samaritan woman to the topic of true worship and the Samaritan nation. What accounts for this seemingly disconnected switch? The answer is John's treatment of
the biblical prophetic tradition about the northern kingdom
of Samaria, that is, the first Jacob-Israel of which the woman
and her fellow Samaritans constitute a remnant. When the
woman perceives that Jesus is a prophet, John is probably making Jesus take on the mantle of the prophet Jeremiah.[11] Like

10. Hugo Odeberg's statement about those who have been born "from above"
is relevant: "He who has been born from above and entered the spiritual world
and eternal life, he will himself be a source of eternal, spiritual life. The all-
inclusiveness of the spiritual world implies that all spiritual beings partake in the
eternal generation of life, *hudōr hallomenon eis zōēn aiōnion*, that proceeds from
God" (*Fourth Gospel*, 169).

11. And not the prophet like Moses of Deut 18:18, as some commentators
think, e.g., W. A. Meeks, *The Prophet-King, Novum Testamentum Supplement* 14 (Leiden, 1967), 34; R. E. Brown, *The Gospel According to John I-XII*, AB (New York,
1966), 171. The woman refers to *a* prophet, not to *the* prophet. In rabbinic
sources, Jeremiah was identified with the prophet like Moses in Deut 18:18, e.g.,
Midrash Tehillim 1:1. See D. C. Allison, *The New Moses: A Matthean Typology* (Minneapolis, 1993), 53–62.

that prophet, Jesus addresses himself to the Samaritans' departure from the true religion of the Jews.

Jeremiah recalls the early history of God's relationship with Israel (Samaria) in terms of a bridegroom with a bride (Jer 2:2). Israel, however, becoming a harlot, has been unable to restrain her thirst for lovers (Jer 2:20–25) and has forsaken her fountain of living waters, namely, God. Strikingly, just as Jeremiah depicts God as both bridegroom and creator, so John depicts Jesus in his encounter with the Samaritan woman in the same way. Thus Jesus links the woman's past love life and the need for her to return to a divine fountain of living water.

The explicit parallel in John's Gospel (Jn 4:12) between Jacob and Jesus—"Art thou [Jesus] greater than our father Jacob?" says the Samaritan woman to Jesus—takes on more meaning in light of John's focus on the topic of worship. Jacob was the father, the creator of the old Samaria; Jesus, the creator of the new Samaria. The beginnings of the first Samaritans was when Jacob met a woman (Rachel) at the well, just as the beginnings of the new Samaritans is when Jesus meets a woman at this same well. Jeremiah had indicated that an act of re-creation was required for the transformation of the old Samaria (Israel). Jesus proves to be the agent of just such a transformation in producing the new Samaria.

The fruitfulness and multiplication among the Samaritans is of a figurative, higher order and is to be contrasted with the fate of the lower order of creation. The Samaritans arrive at their elevated position because they are convinced that their previous path to salvation, their state before re-creation, was imperfect. In the lower creation, if human beings reproduce and the child who results suffers an illness that threatens death, the imperfection requires attention. In typical fashion John turns to just such an aspect of the lower creation.

Just after his interaction with the Samaritans—and we would want to know why there is a switch to such an apparently different topic—Jesus heals a nobleman's son. By doing so, he restores the blessing of fruitfulness to the parent. John draws attention to the fact that geographically Jesus has returned to

Cana of Galilee "where he made the water wine" (Jn 4:46).
That incident was about the marriage of a couple, the prelim-
inary stage to the birth of children. In other words, while John
focuses on the healing of the child, he also manages to allude
to the larger picture of marriage and reproduction. His motivation is to set out a plain parallel to the creation of the male
and the female on day six of creation and the blessing on them
to produce offspring. Philo too draws a link between human
reproduction and God's creation of the world: "Parents, in my
opinion, are to their children what God is to the world, since
just as he achieved existence for the non-existent, so they in
imitation of his power, as far as they are capable, immortalize
the race" (*De Leg.* 2.225, cp. *Det.* 54, *Mos.* 2.209).

John states that the healing of the nobleman's son is the
second miracle that Jesus did. The first was the changing of
water into wine at Cana. The notion of procreation is central
to each miracle. The disciples believe in Jesus because of the
miracle with the wine. The miracle is about his "hour,"
namely, the hour of his death followed by his rebirth. Their
belief signifies that they are his offspring, the branches of the
vine. The nobleman's son experiences a passage from death to
life, and the nobleman and his household come to believe in
Jesus. Presumably they too are offspring of Jesus in a sense
similar to how the disciples (and the Samaritans) become offspring.

Four, in Genesis food for the human creations of day six was
to consist in the harvest of the earth. In John, when the disciples return to Jesus with food, after he has brought about the
re-creation of the Samaritan woman, he launches into a discourse about a different kind of harvesting of food. The many
Samaritans who are coming to accept him as Messiah, because
of the woman's testimony, are equated with a harvest.[12] The

---

12. For the personification of a piece of food as the Messiah, the *aphikoman,*
"The Coming One," the piece of food eaten on Passover Eve and at the Last
Supper, see Robert Eisler, "Das Letzte Abendmahl," *ZNW* 24 (1925), 161–92;

discourse is an allegorization of the harvest of day six of creation. Immediately noteworthy is that in Jesus' reference to food
the term used is *brōsis* and not *brōma* which would give the more
natural meaning.[13] The term used in Jn 4:34 is the one used
in Gen 1:29 about food to serve the needs of all creatures. Also
noteworthy is that the language Jesus employs about food has
close association with reproduction, the very topic that John
has just focused on.[14] In giving expression to the implied transformation of the Samaritans into new beings because of their
newly acquired knowledge, Jesus employs the language of sowing and harvesting. Philo compares food, in the form of plants
and trees, to the mind and what has been sown and planted
in it (*De Agric.* 8–10).

The ordinary fact that the disciples have returned with food
has obviously inspired the figurative language about the Samaritans as a harvest. We would still wish to know, however,
why so much attention is devoted to this agricultural aspect.
The focus on the administration of food on the sixth day of
creation provides the solution.[15] When John has Jesus state that
his food is to do the will of God and to accomplish his work
(Jn 4:34), the work is that of creation. Indeed, the verb used
is *teleioō* ("to complete") and the notion is that Jesus brings to
completion the work of creation, precisely the notion that
dominates so far John's presentation of all the work of Jesus.[16]
It is the same work that he is about to do, as we shall shortly

David Daube, *He That Cometh* (London, 1966); and D. B. Carmichael, "David
Daube on the Eucharist and the Passover Seder," *JSNT* 42 (1991), 45–67.

13. See Birger Olsson, *Structure and Meaning in the Fourth Gospel* (Lund, 1974),
221.

14. On one aspect of how harvesting comes to be a metaphor for the production of human beings, see C. M. Carmichael, " 'Treading' in the Book of Ruth,"
ZAW 92 (1980), 248–66.

15. In Philo's discussion of Noah as the first tiller of the soil, when he planted
the first vineyard, Philo states that agriculture began with Noah and on the third
day of creation (*Ques Gen* 2.66).

16. Cp. Schnackenburg, *St John*, 1:447, 452.

note, even on the sabbath day along with his father, God, who works on that day (Jn 5:16–18).

When Jesus describes his work among the Samaritans in terms of sowing and harvesting, it is possible to pinpoint precisely how this work is thought of as a process comparable to the way food at the time of the creation of the world came into existence. That food was characterized by Philo in the following terms: "And, after a fashion quite contrary to the present order of Nature, all were laden with fruit as soon as ever they came into existence. For now the processes take place in turn, one at one time, one at another, not all of them simultaneously at one season" (*De Opic.* 40, 41). Jesus suggests that a comparable miracle is occurring among the Samaritans: "Say not ye, There are yet four months, and then cometh harvest? behold, I say unto you, Lift up your eyes, and look on the fields; for they are white already to harvest" (Jn 4:35). Jesus contrasts the normally experienced time difference between sowing and harvest with what happens to the Samaritans, namely, the entire process takes place at one time.[17] The felicitous consequence is that sower and reaper are able to rejoice together. This joy is both an expression of the completed order of creation, to wit, the spontaneous abundance of the sixth day of creation, and a celebration of the births that the Baptist anticipated in his role as the friend of the bridegroom.

Like Jesus, interpreting to his disciples the topic of creation, Rabbi Simlai, a Palestinian *Amoraite* of the third century, interprets Gen 1:26, "Let us make man in our image, after our likeness," to his disciples. The statement, according to Simlai, means that the man, the woman, and the divine Spirit jointly produce offspring (*Gen. Rabba* 8:9). Jesus, the woman, and the divine Spirit accomplish this task precisely in accordance with the injunction of Gen 1:26.[18]

17. For a rabbinic parallel to the notion that one day in the future the earth will be sown and bear fruit in one and the same day, see *Torath Kohanim Behukothai*, M. M. Kasher, *Encyclopedia of Biblical Interpretation* (New York, 1953), 1: no. 163, 42.

18. G. F. Moore thinks that Rabbi Simlai's interpretation was directed against

Following through on his focus on the joy that is appropriate at the harvesting of the Samaritans, Jesus quotes a proverb, "And herein is that saying true, One soweth, and another reapeth" (Jn 4:37). Commentators note that the saying in its usual application refers to a distressing situation, but Jesus, who is aware of this usual application, is able to achieve the opposite effect.[19] There is thus an intended surprise in the words, "And herein is that saying true": a situation of joy, not trouble, has been established because there is a newly transformed state of nature that is similar to what occurred at creation.

Elsewhere in John there is a parallel to his thinking about trouble and joy in the saying about one sowing and another reaping. In Jn 16:21 there is the explicit contrast between trouble and joy, precisely in regard to the topic of human fruitfulness: the hour during which a woman gives birth is one of travail followed by joy. Jesus is the one speaking about this aspect of human birth and, as when he addresses his disciples about the Samaritans, his intention is to direct his disciples to the new order of creation.

There is also a rabbinic parallel. In *Gen. Rabba* 42:3 Rabbi Samuel ben Nahman engages in a semantic exercise in regard to the story of creation. He draws a distinction between the expression, "And it came to pass," and "And it shall come to pass." The former denotes trouble, the latter joy. The former expression is used in descriptions of the days of creation in Genesis, for example, "And evening came to pass and morning came to pass, a sixth day." Rabbi Samuel argues that, contrary

---

Christians as heretics, in *Judaism in the First Centuries of the Christian Era: The Age of the Tannaim* (Cambridge, Mass., 1966), 1:366 n. 4. I think it more likely that both John and Rabbi Simlai are interpreting the enigmatic reference to "us" in Gen 1:26 as alluding to maleness and femaleness in the godhead (see Rabbi Samuel's view in note 20 below). Simlai's apparent reference to an ordinary man and an ordinary woman makes no sense in that they have not yet come into being. The focus is on those (heavenly) beings who produced the first man, or rather the first male-female. The sexuality of the Samaritan woman may stand for femaleness that has to be, and is, transformed by heavenly water into divine female sexuality.

19. C. K. Barrett, *The Gospel According to St. John* (London, 1955), 203.

to his opponents' view, these days were not occasions for joy because they lacked completion. As proof of the future, completed order of creation, he cites Zech 14:8, "And it shall come to pass in that day, that living waters shall go out from Jerusalem." His views constitute a remarkable echo of those that John has Jesus express. In Jesus' discussion with the Samaritan woman there is reference to living waters and the role of Jerusalem. Even should there be, as is likely, no connection between the two sources, we can still see how the creation story was treated at a time later than John's Gospel.[20]

20. Samuel was a Palestinian *Amoraite* of the earlier part of the third century. Similar to Jesus' contrast between worship at Jerusalem and worship of God in spirit and truth, Samuel directed attention away from supplicating at the ruined site of the Temple in Jerusalem to seeking the (female) *Shechinah* in heaven. His view was contrary to that of those who believed that the divine presence still abided at the ruined site. He was interested in the notion of androgyny: the union of the male and the female in the first man. He thought of God as possessing both male and female characteristics. His Messianic interests were also unconventional. He speculated about an Ephraimite Messiah from the tribe of Joseph. See Moore, *Judaism* 1:369, 453, 2:204, 352, 370–71. The Samaritan woman refers to the Messiah (Jn 4:25). From a Samaritan perspective it seems reasonable to assume that their Messiah would be linked to Ephraim. They traced their own descent from Ephraim, son of Joseph.

Chapter 9

Day Seven

(Gen 2:1–3) [1]Thus the heavens and the earth were finished, and all the host of them. [2]And on the seventh day God ended his work which he had made; and he rested on the seventh day from all his work which he had made. [3]And God blessed the seventh day, and sanctified it: because that in it he had rested from all his work which God created and made.

(Jn 5:1–47) [1]After this there was a feast of the Jews; and Jesus went up to Jerusalem. [2]Now there is at Jerusalem by the sheep market a pool, which is called in the Hebrew tongue Bethesda, having five porches. [3]In these lay a great multitude of impotent folk, of blind, halt, withered, waiting for the moving of the water. [4]For an angel went down at a certain season into the pool and troubled the water: whosoever then first after the troubling of the water stepped in was made whole of whatsoever disease he had. [5]And a certain man was there, which had an infirmity thirty and eight years. [6]When Jesus saw him lie, and knew that he had been now a long time in that case, he saith unto him, Wilt thou be made whole? [7]The impotent man answered him, Sir, I have no man, when the water is troubled, to put me into the pool: but while I am coming, another steppeth down before me. [8]Jesus saith unto him, Rise, take up thy bed, and walk. [9]And immediately the man was made whole, and took up his bed, and walked: and on the same day was the sabbath.

[10]The Jews therefore said unto him that was cured, It is the sabbath day: it is not lawful for thee to carry thy bed. [11]He answered them, He that made me whole, the same said unto me, Take up thy bed, and walk. [12]Then asked they him, What man is that which said unto thee, Take up thy bed, and walk?

[13]And he that was healed wist not who it was: for Jesus had conveyed himself away, a multitude being in that place. [14]Afterward Jesus findeth him in the temple, and said unto him, Behold, thou art made whole: sin no more, lest a worse thing come unto thee. [15]The man departed, and told the Jews that it was Jesus, which had made him whole. [16]And therefore did the Jews persecute Jesus, and sought to slay him, because he had done these things on the sabbath day.

[17]But Jesus answered them, My father worketh hitherto, and I work. [18]Therefore the Jews sought the more to kill him, because he not only had broken the sabbath, but said also that God was his father, making himself equal with God. [19]Then answered Jesus and said unto them, Verily, verily, I say unto you, The Son can do nothing of himself, but what he seeth the father do: for what things soever he doeth, these also doeth the Son likewise. [20]For the Father loveth the Son, and sheweth him all things that himself doeth: and he will shew him greater works than these, that ye may marvel. [21]For as the Father raiseth up the dead, and quickeneth them; even so the Son quickeneth whom he will. [22]For the Father judgeth no man, but hath committed all judgement unto the Son: [23]That all men should honour the Son, even as they honour the Father. He that honoureth not the Son honoureth not the Father which hath sent him. [24]Verily, verily, I say unto you, He that heareth my word, and believeth on him that sent me, hath everlasting life, and shall not come into condemnation; but is passed from death unto life. [25]Verily, verily, I say unto you, The hour is coming, and now is, when the dead shall hear the voice of the Son of God: and they that hear shall live.

[26]For as the Father hath life in himself; so hath he given to the Son to have life in himself; [27]And hath given him authority to execute judgement also, because he is the Son of man. [28]Marvel not at this: for the hour is coming in which all that are in the graves shall hear his voice, [29]And shall come forth; they that have done good, unto the resurrection of life; and they that have done evil, unto the resurrection of damnation. [30]I can of mine own self do nothing: as I hear, I judge: and my judgement is just; because I seek not mine own will, but the will of the Father which hath sent me. [31]If I bear witness of myself, my witness is not true.

[32]There is another that beareth witness of me; and I know that the witness that he witnesseth of me is true. [33]Ye sent unto John, and he bare witness unto the truth. [34]But I receive not testimony from man: but these things I say, that ye might be saved. [35]He was a burning and a shining light: and ye were willing for a season to rejoice in his light.

[36]But I have greater witness than that of John: for the works which the Father hath given me to finish, the same works that I do, bear witness of me, that the Father hath sent me. [37]And the Father himself, which hath sent me, hath borne witness of me. Ye have neither heard his voice at any time, nor seen his shape. [38]And ye have not his word abiding in you: for whom he hath sent, him ye believe not.

[39]Search the Scriptures; for in them ye think ye have eternal life: and they are they which testify of me. [40]And ye will not come to me, that ye might have life. [41]I receive not honour from men. [42]But I know you, that ye have not the love of God in you. [43]I am come in my Father's name, and ye receive me not: if another shall come in his own name, him ye will receive. [44]How can ye believe, which receive honour one of another, and seek not the honour that cometh from God only? [45]Do not think that I will accuse you to the Father: there is one that accuseth you, even Moses, in whom ye trust. [46]For had ye believed Moses, ye would have believed me: for he wrote of me. [47]But if ye believe not his writings, how shall ye believe my words?

Day seven in Genesis about God's rest from work on his creation concerns the institution of the sabbath. The next section of John's Gospel shares a similar concern because it primarily focuses on Jesus' attitude to the sabbath. Despite this obvious link between Gen 2:1–3 and John 5, there is nonetheless a problem. It is far from easy to observe how the theme of the seventh day in Genesis is in effect further played out in this part of the Fourth Gospel. The reason is that John presents the, at first sight, bewildering view that Jesus imitates God in actually working on the sabbath. Consequently, the correspondence between the substance of the Genesis account of the sabbath, when God rested from his work, and John's account is necessarily not straightforward. How then has John proceeded? A number of possible correlations present themselves for consideration.

First, John has kept up his focus on the need for the world to be renewed. That is the reason why Jesus has to work on the sabbath and why the major incident in focus concerns human illness. When his opponents accuse him of making himself equal with God (Jn 5:18), one implication is that Jesus has powers equal to those of God when he worked on the creation of the world. Jesus does what his father does. Consequently, he plays a role comparable to his father's at the creation of the world.

In Jesus' response to his opponents, he states that to hear his words is to have eternal life (Jn 5:24). The implication is that these words are as powerful as the pronouncements at creation that gave life to the universe. What is happening as he speaks is that the climax of the new creation, its sabbath, is at hand. The dead are about to rise from their graves (Jn 5:28, 29).

Second, according to the description of day four of creation in Genesis 1, the sabbath was to constitute a sign and a unit of time, namely, a day. In Exod 31:16, 17 the sabbath is explicitly referred to as a sign. For the pre-Johannine author of Jubilees the sabbath day constitutes a sign of all of God's works of creation, not just the seventh day. This may be John's view too. He refers to how Jesus discourses on the works which God has given him to complete (Jn 5:36, *teleioō* as in the LXX of Gen 2:2). The works are those of creation. When John describes the healing of the invalid on the sabbath, he includes references to signs, seasons, days, and years, the features of the universe that came into existence on the fourth day of creation. John thus provides details about how there was a feast of the Jews, without any reference as to which significant one it might be, and to the thirty-eight years that the invalid had been waiting for a cure. He also refers to the season at which the sick went into the pool of water.

Third, according to another view of the author of the Book

of Jubilees (1:29)—a view that emerges in his vision of the end of time—the luminaries of the fourth day of creation that determine the signs, seasons, days, and years constitute instruments of healing. The same view is shared by the author of Revelation (Rev 22:2–5). In his vision of the new Jerusalem a life-giving river—the river of Eden—contains the tree of life (of Gen 2:9, 10) that bears fruit for each month of the year. The leaves of the tree serve a curative function. When healing has been accomplished, the city will no longer need the luminaries of the fourth day of creation. The vision has been inspired by the prophet Isaiah, who describes Jerusalem's (Zion's) future as a time when the everlasting light of the Glory of God will replace the light of the sun and the moon (Isa 60: 19, 20). John's focus on human illness—in a setting that is the old Jerusalem—may share the eschatological perspective that emerges in the author of Revelation's account of the new creation (Rev 22:2–5).

Fourth, the use of features that belong to the other days of creation in setting out a particular day is, as has been noted many times, a typical strategy of John and would complement the view that the sabbath celebrates all the works of creation. The fig tree in the incident with Nathanael, John's second day of creation, belongs to the third day of creation. The doves, oxen, and sheep that Jesus expels from the Temple and that figure in John's fourth day of creation belong to days five and six of creation.[1] The human beings who need to be cured of illness and whose first ancestors came into existence on the sixth day of creation receive attention on John's seventh day. Philo comments on this aspect of the creation story, namely, that the elements of each day of creation show up on other days: "To each of the days He assigned some of the portions of the whole" (*De Opic.*15).

---

1. The mention of the animals that Jesus beats up is found only in John's Gospel, possibly again to be explained by John's immersion in all the details of the creation story.

In his seventh day John returns not just to features of the fourth and sixth days of creation, but he also goes back to features of the fifth day. He records an incident in which broken-down persons need to place themselves in a pool of water to make themselves whole again. While such an incident serves to highlight the imperfection of the present created order, the incident also enables John to complement his allegorical interpretation of the fifth day of the Genesis creation story.

The fifth day in Genesis 1 is about the creation of water creatures. John has already used this feature for allegorical purposes. He interprets the Baptist as having brought about new beings by the use of water. John turns again to the use of water and, in this instance, pursues the literal equivalent to the allegorical water creatures of day five. The water at the pool brings about a physical miracle that transforms a human being from one state to another. The incident occurs at a place in Jerusalem called the Sheep Gate, a pool of water, which has five entrances. (I am not suggesting that the detail about the number five is intended to direct attention to day five of creation.)

The broken-down human beings who attempt to heal themselves by using this pool are, so we might infer, like the people who come to the Baptist at the water of Aenon. They come to repent of their previous life and become new beings. This link between the two episodes would explain why a reference to the crippled man's sinfulness comes into focus ("Behold, thou art made whole: sin no more, lest a worse thing come unto thee" [Jn 5:14]). His outward and inward condition is equivalent to the state of sinfulness that induces people to come for baptism in order to become new beings. In the discourse that follows the healing episode Jesus does indeed refer to the Baptist's activity (Jn 5:33–35).

Fifth, the sabbath day rest is the central feature of the seventh day in Genesis 1, but not, it would appear, at least on the surface, of John's description of the sabbath in this section of his Gospel. In Gen 2:1–3 God rested from his work on the seventh day after he had completed the heavens and the earth.

Such is the plain meaning of the Genesis text. Its sophisticated treatment by John involves, certainly on the face of it, the contradictory notion that God continues to work on the sabbath; that is how Jesus justifies his work on it: "My father worketh hitherto, and I work." The view propounded is closely allied to one found in Philo and in some rabbinic circles.

Philo, in effect—from our point of view—explains away the statement that God rested on the seventh day. For Philo, it is impossible that that is the meaning because "God never ceases creating, but as it is the property of fire to burn and of snow to be cold, so it is the property of God to create." Scripture, according to Philo, does not say that God rested. The verb is transitive and active *katepausen,* not the middle *epausato.* The meaning is God caused inferior creative agencies to cease, while He continues to create (*Leg. All.* 1.5, 6, 18; *De Cher.* 87).[2]

Jesus is accused of violating the sabbath because he told the man to carry his bed on that day (Jn 5:10, 12), and he also healed him on the sabbath (Jn 5:15, 16). The criticism reproduces an uninformed view, possibly not a very representitive one, of the type that John attributes to Nicodemus when he communicates that rebirth requires entry into the womb a second time. Informed rabbinic circles could "prove" that God worked. It was simply that he carried no burden beyond his own dwelling, heaven and earth, or to a distance greater than his own stature. His "work" therefore falls within permissible limits (*Exod. Rabba* 39:9). Rabbi Pinchas, about 360 c.e., argues that God rested from work on his world, but not from his work on the wicked, because he shows to them something of their punishment, nor from his work on the righteous, because he shows to them something of their reward (*Gen. Rabba* 11:10).

2. For a discussion of Philo's view, see C. H. Dodd, *The Interpretation of the Fourth Gospel* (Cambridge, Eng., 1965), 320–23. For the rabbinic background about God's continual activity in relation to the works of creation and what the divine sabbath rest meant, see Hugo Odeberg, *The Fourth Gospel Interpreted in Its Relation to Contemporaneous Religious Currents in Palestine and the Hellenistic-Oriental World* (Uppsala, 1929), 201–4.

It is interesting that Jesus introduces the distinction between the cripple's implied new state of righteousness and his previous lack of it ("Sin no more, lest a worse thing come unto thee" [Jn 5:14]). John too may have the view that attending to the man on the sabbath was justified, because God does not cease at any time from attending to a man's moral state.

In regard to healing on the sabbath, *b. Yom.* 85a-b states, "If circumcision [carried out on the eighth day], which affects one of our 248 members supersedes the Sabbath, how much more must the whole body supersede the Sabbath." Rabbi Eliezer, around 90 C.E., states, "Circumcision supersedes the Sabbath. Why? Because on its account one makes oneself guilty of annihilating the Torah if it is not carried out at the appointed time. And is not an inference from the less to the greater permissible? For the sake of one member he supersedes the Sabbath, and shall not the whole of him supersede the Sabbath?" (*t. Shab.* 15, 16). To resolve this conflict of laws between the requirement of circumcision and the observance of the sabbath the rabbis give precedence to the needs of the body. Should these require attention on the sabbath the work has to be done. John's description of the Jesuanic position is similar.

For Philo the health of the body is dependent on "respite from continuous and wearisome toil" on the seventh day of the week (*De Leg.* 2.260). Presumably for John, where there is no health, as in the examples of those at the Bethesda pool, healing has to take place before the issue of rest from work on the sabbath can be raised.

Sixth, as is to be expected in John, there are subtle links between his presentation of the life of Jesus and his use of Scripture, in this instance, Gen 2:1–3. In John's account there are allusions to the theme of rest, the notion central to the original account of the institution of the sabbath. These allusions are intended to demonstrate that Jesus must work on the sabbath because God's true rest for his creation has not yet been achieved. The work of Jesus is to heal the imperfections manifest in the material order of creation. This is why he heals the man on the sabbath. When the healing waters of the pool, into which the sick are placed, are at rest healing does not take place. When they are troubled healing does take place.[3] The disjunction—waters at rest, no healing of the sick—possibly draws attention to the fact that a true rest for the creation still awaits.

On the other occasions in John when he uses the verb *tarassō* ("to trouble"), the reference is to a state of trouble because of the approach of death, or of the fact of death itself (Jn 11: 33, 12:27; 13:21; 14:1, 27). In the context about the troubled waters, there may be an implication that any healing brought about by them is inadequate because the person still has to confront his or her death. The problem of those in the grave is taken up in the next part of John's discussion (Jn 5:25–29). Already in the biblical proverbial tradition there is an association between the idea of a rest and physical death (e.g., Job 3:13, 17). We may be observing in John the same contrast between trouble and joy similar to the rabbinic notion, already commented on, about how the original days of creation were not occasions for joy because they lacked completion.

Another allusion to the Genesis theme of a rest in the created order occurs in Jn 5:25, "Truly, truly, I say to you, the hour is coming, and now is, when the dead will hear the voice of the Son of God, and those who hear will live." Jesus links the eschatological rest that is coming with the work he is presently doing in order to achieve this true rest.[4] Jesus alludes to the fact that many people are presently in their graves, that is,

3. Textual evidence and the non-Johannine language are indications that v. 4 (about the descent of an angel) is an addition; see R. E. Brown, *The Gospel According to John I–XII*, AB (New York, 1966), 207. The meaning of the verse also conflicts with John's argument in this section. John contrasts the healing brought about by the activity of the waters with the healing effected by Jesus. This contrast would be lost if an angel of God were introduced. The implied contrast between the waters at rest and the waters astir supports, however, the retention of the clause in v. 3 about the people waiting for the movement of the waters. The clause in v. 3 (found in the Western MS tradition) has a textual history different from v. 4.

4. Cp. Harold Weiss, "The Sabbath in the Fourth Gospel," *JBL* 110 (1991) 311–21.

are at "rest" there. The implication is again that this kind of rest is not consistent with, indeed it is antagonistic to, the true order of creation, which is to be restored by the resurrection. The present, unsatisfactory state of rest in the material order of creation again supports Jesus' view that he must work on the sabbath.[5]

Seventh, and finally, at the end of the discussion on the sabbath John refers to Jesus' interpretation of the writings of Moses. In particular, there is a reference to a study of these writings. On the one hand, the implication may be that the dispute about working on the seventh day revolves around the issue about how the institution of the sabbath at the creation of the world has to be understood.[6] On the other hand, the reference may equally well include the interpretation of all the days of creation. Moses, for John, is the one who wrote the story of creation in Genesis 1.

However we understand the statement about the writings of Moses—and these writings include the creation story—at the very least it encourages an interpretive approach that I have pursued. John uses the creation story to convey the cosmological significance of the deeds of Jesus. As we have observed, Philo reveals a parallel mode of thinking. His view is that, whereas contemplative pagans got so far in comprehending the nature of the creator from the created universe, a full disclosure was given to the Jewish nation through the writings of Moses (*Leg. All.* 3.97–103; *De Praem.* 46).

I have argued that from the opening of John's Gospel to the end of chapter 5 there is a complex and ornate replication of

5. Dodd, *Interpretation*, 324, is consequently wrong when he states that the question of the sabbath is forgotten by John at this point in his discourse.

6. The notion that Moses in the form of his writings accuses Jesus' opponents is reminiscent of the rabbinic use of the device of hypostatization. A document from which parts have been unfairly omitted takes up its own defense, speaks out, and attacks the culprit. The use of the device in regard to biblical texts, for example, by Simeon ben Jochai in the second century C.E., can be traced to Hellenistic rhetorical instruction. See David Daube, "Two Cases of Hypostatizing," *Talmudic Law*, ed. C. M. Carmichael (Berkeley, 1992), 377–80.

the seven days of creation in Genesis 1. Such a scheme would not be an isolated example in first century Hellenistic Jewish and Christian circles. From this period of time there are apocalyptic and other works (for example, the Apocalypse of Abraham 17–19; 2 Enoch 33; and the Wisdom of Solomon), which interpret history or its end as a series of seven great days or weeks. At the heart of eschatology, the study of the final events of human history, is the view that the end of the historical order will replicate its beginning. For an evangelist of the first century to view the history of Jesus from the perspective of creation is therefore natural, even obligatory. As N. A. Dahl well demonstrates, because the early Christians thought of Jesus as bringing renewal at the end of time, they necessarily linked his life and its consequences to the creation.[7]

John's Gospel opens with creation motifs and moves on to the issue of the sabbath and the seventh day of creation in Chapter 5. So much is obvious to any reader. Less clear are the connections between the details of the account of creation in Genesis 1 and the ins and outs of the material spanning the opening of the Gospel to the end of chapter 5. Some links are more suggestive than others. Of these I would cite the following sequences of material in John 1–5 and Genesis 1.

The curious emphasis in Jn 1:19–28 on the negative role of the Baptist suggests the void of day one of creation. The descent of the Spirit like a dove on the water (Jn 1:32) recalls the Spirit that hovered over the face of the primeval waters on the same day.[8] The turning of two of the Baptist's disciples to Jesus with whom they spend "that day" (Jn 1:39) suggests their exposure to the light that was called day in Gen 1:5, because Jesus personifies the light of day one. The promised opening

7. N. A. Dahl, *Jesus in the Memory of the Early Church* (Minneapolis, 1976), 120–40.

8. Of this particular link between the Spirit at creation and a dove, we now know that it is pre-Christian because the same analogy has turned up in a recent fragment of the Dead Sea Scrolls. See D. C. Allison, "The Baptism of Jesus and a New Dead Sea Scroll," *BAR* 18 (1992), 58–60.

of the heavens to Nathanael in Jn 1:51 points to the firmament
of the heavens on day two in Genesis. The miracle of water
turned into wine in Jn 2:1–11 points to the water and the earth
that yields fruit on day three in Genesis. The detailed interest
in signs, seasons, days, and years in the violent incident at the
Temple (Jn 2:13–25) relates back to their appearance on day
four of creation. The Baptist's use of water to produce converts
(Jn 3:23) is reminiscent of the creation of the water creatures
on day five. Finally, the strange encounter between Jesus and
the Samaritan woman, and her conversion of her fellow Samaritans to belief in him as the Messiah (Jn 4:1–32), recall the
role of the male and the female on day six of creation and
their potential fruitfulness in reproducing their own kind.

For other links that appear more speculative I remind the
reader of the necessity of putting on first-century spectacles,
especially those of someone like Philo, to appreciate how John
read Scripture in his time. John combined a plain and allegorical reading of Scripture that is part of his religious culture to
produce a similar reading of the life of Jesus. His method is, I
have argued, the key to understanding the many links between
John's Gospel and Genesis 1.

Index of Sources

References are to the numbering in the English versions.

BIBLICAL SOURCES

Genesis		2:7	2, 30
1:1–5	37, 41, 54	2:9, 10	119
1:1–10	28	2:19	2, 30
1:1—2:3	3, 29	3:19	17
1:1—2:4	26	3:22	27
1:2	22, 44–45, 63	6—9	38
1:2–5	23	22:16	24
1:5	51, 125	25:27	65
1:6–8	56–58, 60	28:10–17	59
1:7	57, 63	28:12	60
1:9–13	67, 69, 96	28:12–15	64
1:11	63	29:7	105
1:11–13	70, 96	Exodus	
1:12	17, 71	1:7	18, 20
1:14	81, 84, 86	3:14	14
1:14–19	79, 84	3:18	15
1:16	3, 23, 51	3:20	5
1:20	91	4:23	15
1:20–23	90, 98	5:1	13, 15
1:21	17	5:3	15
1:22	29	5:5	13, 15
1:24–31	94, 99–103	5:9	13
1:26	112–113	7:9, 10	17
1:28	18, 20, 29, 104	7:24	20
1:29	18, 20, 111	8:1, 8, 20	15
1:29—2:3	21	8:22	19
2—11	2	8:25–29	15
2:1–3	115–17, 120, 122	9:1, 13	15
		9:14, 16	19
2:2	118	9:18, 23	20

Exodus (*cont.*)

9:29	19
10:3, 7–9	15
10:9	13
10:15	17
10:21–23	23
10:21–29	18
10:24–26	15
12	15
12:2	81
12:31	15
13	15
14:31	17
15	21
15:23	20
16:4	20–21
16:15	20
18:8–12	15
19	11, 30
19:4	22
20:4, 7	28
20:8–11	27
20:11	12
20:18–21	30
25:1	3, 37
27:20—30:10	37
29:38	49
30:11, 17, 22, 34	3, 37
31	7, 25
31:1	3, 37
31:2–11	26
31:12–17	3, 37
31:16	118
31:17	7, 118
32	7–13, 21, 24–26
32:1	16
32:4	11, 13, 16, 27
32:5	12–13
32:11–13	24
32:12, 13	25
32:24	16
32:27	13
34:10	5
34:28	28
39:1—40:33	3

Leviticus

11:9–19	96
19:23–25	63

Numbers

21:6–9	87
21:8, 9	88

24:7	91
28:3	49

Deuteronomy

4:13	28
4:15–19	23
4:32	5
5:12–15	16, 27
10:4	28
14:9–20	96
16:1–8	81
18:15	43
18:18	43, 108
21:16	11
24:5	95
32:11	22, 45
32:12	22
34:12	17

1 Kings

7:25, 44	8
12:25–33	8

2 Chronicles

4:4, 15	8
29—30	81

Job

3:13, 17	123
31:26–28	4
38:5—8	71

Psalms

19:2	8
19:8	61
29:3	8
78:42	17
104:2	47
104:3, 4	66
104:14, 15	71
104:19	81
106:20	8
108:6	8
128:3	74
136	5

Proverbs

5:15	105, 107
5:18	105
9:17	105–106

Canticles

4:12	106

Isaiah

6:3	8
40:3	43
40:12	71
40:12–14	4
40:12–31	43

Isaiah (*cont.*)
40:18	22
40:18–23	4
40:18–31	23
40:45	4
41:17–20	5
42:5–17	5
43:15–21	5
45:18	4
51:1, 2	53
51:10	5
60:19, 20	119
66:10	95

Jeremiah
2:2, 20–25	109
4:23	22
10:1–16	4
10:5	22
20:15	95
31:31–37	4
32:17–21	4

Lamentations
2:19	44

Ezekiel
46:13	49

Daniel
8:11–13	49
11:31	49
12:11	49

Hosea
8:6	8
9:10	63–64
12:1–6	65

Amos
9:5–7	4

Zechariah
14:8	114

Matthew
3:1–6	47
3:17	46
4:15	63
4:19	91
11:14	43
12:8	34
16:17, 18	52
17:12	43
26:61	82
28:19	93, 103

Mark
1:2–6	47
1:5, 11	46
1:17	91
2:19	108
2:28	34
9:13	43
14:58	82
16:15	93
16:16	93, 103

Luke
1:17	43
3:1–6	47
3:22	46
6:5	34

John
1:1–18	32
1:3	33, 70
1:6–8	54
1:7	46
1:8	46, 51
1:9	46
1:10	33, 47
1:11	52
1:14	46, 49, 64, 68
1:15	47
1:15–18	54
1:15–42	37, 41
1:18	55
1:19	47
1:19–28	54, 125
1:24	47
1:29	48
1:29–34	54
1:29—2:1	35
1:29—2:12	88
1:30	47
1:31	44
1:32	125
1:33, 34	61
1:36	50
1:39	50–51, 125
1:40–46	104
1:43	63
1:43–51	56, 58
1:45	59, 61
1:48	64
1:49	81
1:51	58, 64, 126
2:1	88
2:1–5	75
2:1–11	126
2:1–12	67
2:4	74–76, 95
2:6	73
2:7	72
2:11	38, 76

John (*cont.*)
2:12	75
2:13–25	126
2:13—3:21	79
2:20	82
2:21	49
2:25	85
3:2	84
3:4	78
3:5, 12	60
3:13	60, 86
3:14	87
3:19–21	85
3:22	94, 102
3:22–36	90–91
3:23	98, 126
3:25	96
3:29	74, 108
3:31–36	97
3:34, 36	97
4:1	102
4:1–3	104
4:1–32	126
4:1–54	99–102
4:2	92, 94, 102
4:6	103
4:7	73
4:12	102, 107, 109
4:14	61
4:15	73
4:18	106
4:19	107
4:25	114
4:27	105
4:34	111
4:35	112
4:35–38	92
4:37	113
4:46	110
4:49–53	70
5	37, 43, 115–17
5:3, 4	123
5:10, 12	121
5:14	120, 122
5:15, 16	121
5:16–18	112
5:16–36	1
5:18, 24	118
5:25–29	123
5:28, 29	118
5:33–35	120
5:36	118

5:46, 47	34
8:12	52, 60
8:23	61
8:48–58	107
9:4	52
9:7	73
11:33	123
12:24	78
12:27	123
12:29	66
13:21	123
14:1, 27	123
14—17	40
15:1–8	76
15:11	95
16:21	75, 95, 113
17:1–4	75
17:5, 24	38
17:13	95
19:25–27	75
19:26	74
20:12	66
21:11	89

Galatians
1:15	75

Ephesians
2:20	53

Colossians
1:16, 17	33

Philemon
1:10	92

Hebrews
1:2	33

1 Peter
1:19, 20	49

Revelation
3:14	33
5:6	103
7:17	48
12:1, 2	86
13	103
13:1, 11	98
14:7, 9, 10	98
17:14	48
17:15	91
19:13, 16	48
21:1—22:5	48
21:14	53
21:22, 23	49, 83, 89
21:27	84
22:2–5	119

APOCRYPHA AND PSEUDEPIGRAPHA
Apocalypse of Abraham
   17—19   40, 125
Barnabus
   6:13   40, 52
2 Baruch
   57:1   91
   57:2   53
1 Enoch
   17:4   57
   54:8   106
   60:15   43
2 Enoch
   30:13   82
   33   40, 125
3 Enoch
   11:1   61
2 Esdras
   6:39   45
   6:41   43, 58, 66
   6:42   71–72
   6:43   70, 72
   6:44   70–72, 86
   6:49   98
   6:58, 59   38
   7:30   52
   16:53–63   62
   16:57, 58   71
Jubilees
   1:27, 28   50
   1:29   87, 119
   2:1–18   66
   2:2   43, 66
   2:3, 5   66
Liber Antiquitatum Biblicarum
  (Pseudo–Philo)
   4.11   53
2 Maccabees
   7:23, 28, 37   18
Sibylline Oracles
   3:24–26   82
Sirach
   50:3   72
   50:7   85
Testament of Naphtali
   5:3–5   85
Wisdom
   13:2   4
   19:6   4, 18
   19:6–8   39
   19:7   70

DEAD SEA SCROLLS
Code of Damascus
   2:8   38
1QSb
   4:25–28   84
RABBINIC SOURCES
Mishnah
  m. (Pirqe) Aboth
   1:12   93
   5:1   29
  m. Baba Metzia
   2:11   93
  m. Baba Qamma
   1:4–5   65
  m. Hullin
   5:5   51
  Mekhilta (of Rabbi
    Ishmael)
   Exodus 16:4   21
   Exodus 18:27   85
Tosephtah
  t. Pesahim
   1:27   61
  t. Shabbath
   15, 16   122
Babylonian Talmud
  b. Berakoth
   32b   54
  b. Erubin
   64b   61
  b. Hagigah
   15a   45
  b. Makkoth
   24b   50
  b. Yebamoth
   22a   92
  b. Yoma
   85a–b   122
Jerusalem Talmud
  y. Abodah Zarah
   40a   61
  y. Hagiga
   77b   45
  y. Taanith
   64b   69
Midrash Rabba
  Genesis Rabba
   1:3   58, 66
   1:4   50, 52, 63
   1:9   50
   2:3   85

Midrash Rabba
  Genesis Rabba (*cont.*)
    2:3   85
    2:5   44
    3:4   47
    3:6   51
    5:1   71
    6:1   81
    6:2   85
    8:9   112
    11:10   121
    12:2   54
    12:6   92
    13:13, 14   69, 106
    42:3   113
    68:18   64
  Exodus Rabba
    1:22   39
    39:9   121
  Leviticus Rabba
    27:2   61
  Numbers Rabba
    8:3   92
Other Midrashim
  Midrash Tehillim
    1:1   108
  Yalkuth
    Numbers 23:9 53
OTHER ANCIENT JEWISH WRITINGS
Josephus
  Antiquitates Judaicae
    2.9.2.205   39
    3.180   83
  Bellum Judaicum
    5.212–14   83
Philo
  De Abrahamo
    18   36, 77
    157, 158   84
  De Agricultura
    8–10   111
  De Cherubim
    87   121
  De Confusione
    190   36, 77
  Quod Deterius Potiori insidiari
    solet
    54   110
  Legum Allegoriae
    1.2   88

    1.5, 6, 18   121
    1.20   88
    2.79   88
    3.97–103   124
    3.163   57
  De Migratione Abrahami
    64, 65   96
  De Mutatione Nominum
    81   64
  De Opificio Mundi
    15   62, 94, 97, 119
    26   88
    27   59
    29   66
    38, 39   70
    40   70, 112
    41   112
    44   78
    45, 46, 53–57 85
    55   82, 83
    58   82
    59   86
    68   104
    82   59
    147   104
  De Plantatione
    15   70
    118   82
  De Praemiis et Poenis
    46   124
  Questiones et Solutiones
    in Genesin
    2.47   70, 86
    2.51   38
    2.66   71, 111
    3.49   64
    4.215   59
  Questiones et Solutiones in
    Exodum
    1.9   84
    2.46   107
  Quis Rerum Divinarum Heres
    130–32   97
    132   97, 104
    215   97
  De Somniis
    1.135   97
  De Specialibus Legibus
    2.225   110
    2.260   122
    4.110–12   96

Philo (*cont.*)
  De Vita Mosis
    1.202   70
    2.209   110
    2.267   21

OTHER SOURCES
Corpus Hermeticum
    1.24–26   65
Origen
  Commentarii in Jn 3:34
    3:34   97

Subject Index

Aaron, 7–17, 21–26, 37, 85, 92
Abraham, 24–25, 53, 64, 91, 107
Adam and Eve, 2, 26–29
Allegory, 36–37, 40, 42, 45–46, 51, 57, 60, 63, 77, 82, 91, 98, 102–4, 111, 120
Apostasy, 3, 4, 7–17, 21–27
Atrahasis, 2

Babylonian mathematics, 5
Basilides, 58

Contraception, 10
Conversion, 92–94
Cosmology, 5, 8–10, 19–21, 40, 53, 60, 69, 74, 82–83, 85–88, 98, 124

Decalogue, 7, 11, 26–31

Enuma Elish, 2, 3
Etiological narratives, 1, 9, 11
Exodus and re-creation, 4–5, 18–21, 30, 39, 70

Gematria, 82
Gender, 69–70, 105–6, 113–14
Geographical symbolism, 63, 73, 109–10
Gnosis, 10, 36, 44, 57–58, 60, 87
Golden calf, 7–17, 21–26

Heracleon, 73
Hezekiah, 81
Hippolyt, 87

Jacob, 59, 64–65, 85, 102–3, 105–9
Jeremiah, 108–9
Jeroboam, 8, 10
John the Baptist, 33–34, 43–52, 54, 58–59, 74, 92–98, 102–5, 108, 112, 120

Logos, 33, 37–38, 45, 88

Marduk, 3
Medicine, 20, 87, 119, 122
Memphite cosmogony, 22
Merkabah mysticism, 36
Mesopotamian creation myth, 24
Metatron, 61
Modern theories of creation, 1

Number symbolism, 82, 89

Ophitic sect, 87
Origins, 1, 7, 11, 24–26, 40, 125

Passover, 15, 81, 110
Peratae, 87
Personification, 22, 43, 60, 85, 110, 124, 125
Plato, 36, 47, 49
Power of language, 12–13, 22–23, 28–31, 52, 70, 118
Procreation, 18, 75–78, 86, 92–96, 106, 109–10
Ptah, 22
Purification, 69, 96–97

Resurrection, 10, 75–76, 78, 83, 93, 95, 118, 123–124

Sabbath, 2, 3, 7, 12–16, 21, 25–28, 30, 34, 37, 117–25
Scripture, 34–37, 46, 59–60, 64, 104, 121–22, 124–26
Self-understood, 6
Sexuality and Jesus, 105–8, 112

Shechinah, 114
Sumerian creation myth, 24

Temple, 3, 8–9, 25–26, 37, 47–50, 53–54, 81–84, 87, 89, 114
Timaeus, 36
Time, 51, 88–89

Valentinus, 58